W9-DHN-844

Holt

ELEMENTARY SCIENCE

Joseph Abruscato   Joan Wade Fossaceca
Jack Hassard   Donald Peck

HOLT, RINEHART AND WINSTON, PUBLISHERS
New York • Toronto • London • Sydney

THE AUTHORS

Joseph Abruscato
Associate Dean
College of Education and Social Services
University of Vermont
Burlington, Vermont

Joan Wade Fossaceca
Teacher
Pointview Elementary School
Westerville City Schools
Westerville, Ohio

Jack Hassard
Professor
College of Education
Georgia State University
Atlanta, Georgia

Donald Peck
Supervisor of Science
Woodbridge Township School District
Woodbridge, New Jersey

Editorial Development   William N. Moore, Lois Eskin, Roger R. Rogalin, Stuart M. Natof
Editorial Processing   Margaret M. Byrne, Regina Chilcoat, Shelley L. Feiler, Dorrie K. Berkowitz
Art and Production   Vivian Fenster, Fred C. Pusterla, Robin Swenson, **Russell Dian,** Paula Darmofal, Anita E. Dickhuth
Product Managers   Ronald E. Suchodolski, John W. M. Cooke
Advisory Board   John Boynton, Max Callahan, Glenn Hartman, Norman Hughes, Albert LeFevre, Douglas Nash, Jon Permar, Dennis Spurgeon
Consultant   John Matejowsky
Researchers   Pamela Floch, Gerard LaVan

Photo and art acknowledgments appear on pages 278 and 279.
Cover photograph by © James H. Carmichael, Jr./The Image Bank.

THE CONSULTANTS

Content Consultants

Edward E. C. Clebsch, Ph.D.
Professor of Botany
University of Tennessee
Knoxville, Tennessee

Jerry Faughn, Ph.D.
Professor of Physics
Eastern Kentucky University
Richmond, Kentucky

Ellen M. Herron, Ph.D.
Assistant Director
Lamont-Doherty Geological Observatory
Palisades, New York

Margaret A. LeMone, Ph.D.
Scientist
National Center for Atmospheric Research
Boulder, Colorado

W. T. Lippincott, Ph.D.
Professor of Chemistry
University of Arizona
Tucson, Arizona

Gary Peterson, D.A.
Assoc. Professor of Biology
South Dakota State University
Brookings, South Dakota

Arne E. Slettebak
Professor of Astronomy
Ohio State University
Columbus, Ohio

Gordon Taylor
Principal
Estey School
Saskatoon, Saskatchewan

Teacher Consultants

Peggy Ann Archacki
Assistant Supervisor of Science
Cleveland Public Schools
Cleveland, Ohio

Thomas L. Beck
Teacher
Evening Street Elementary School
Worthington, Ohio

Lynn T. Cluff
Teacher
Central School
South Burlington, Vermont

Linda Coffey, Ph.D.
Director of Early Childhood/Ed.
Broward County Public Schools
Broward County, Florida

Marcia Lambek
Teacher
School One
Scotch Plains, New Jersey

Carole Rutland
Teacher
Muscogee County Public Schools
Columbus, Georgia

Judy Woodward
Science Advisor
Delevan Science Center
Los Angeles City Schools
Los Angeles, California

Rina Zucker
Teacher
Ashford Elementary School
Houston, Texas

Reading Consultants

Paul Greenfield
Associate Professor
English and Humanities
Dutchess Community College
Poughkeepsie, New York

Judith Linscott Martin
Reading Specialist
Montgomery County Public Schools
Montgomery County, Maryland

Evelyn Mason
Elementary Language Arts Supervisor
Indianapolis Public Schools
Indianapolis, Indiana

PILOT SCHOOLS

We gratefully acknowledge the help of the teachers and students who field-tested portions of the Holt Elementary Science program in the spring of 1977. Their comments and criticisms were used to improve the program. The field teachers were:

Margaret Rodriquez
Encinal School
Morgan Hill, CA

Viola Sando
Murphy School
Stamford, CT

Lenore Ambrose
Palmetto El Sch
Miami, FL

Judy Kaplan
Lake Stevens El Sch
OpaLock, FL

Beth Williams
Laura Childs El Sch
Bloomington, IN

David Allen
Howard C. Reiche Sch
Portland, ME

Stephanie Barnhart
Immac Heart of Mary Sch
Towson, MD

John Cooney
Mill Swan El Sch
Worcester, MA

Eileen Martin
Stearns School
Pittsfield, MA

Phil Maines
Fountain El Sch
Grand Rapids, MI

Olivia McKinney
Vernor El Sch
Detroit, MI

Ellen Stob
Hillcrest El Sch
Grand Rapids, MI

Dennis Davis
Portland El Sch
Richfield, MN

Gary Hawkins
Cambridge El Sch
Cambridge, MN

M. Foster
Green Trails Sch
Chesterfield, MO

A. J. Sullivan
Ferguson Florissant Sch Dist
Ferguson, MO

Rick Ashworth
Choteau School
Choteau, MT

Nancy Ritter
Fort Benton Sch
Ft. Benton, MT

J. Ely
Burgess School
Berlin, NH

Edward Douglas
Sumner El Sch
Camden, NJ

Nancy Hearst
Pennypacher El Sch
Willingboro, NJ

Lee Ferrera
St. Jerome Sch
Brooklyn, NY

Robert Kase
Public School 178
Jamaica, NY

Lois Parker
Bloomfield El Sch
Holcomb, NY

Lorraine Sharp
95th Street School
Niagara Falls, NY

Paul Snyder
93rd Street School
Niagara Falls, NY

Helen Suchy
Theo Roosevelt El Sch
Binghamton, NY

Edward Wianecki
School 43
Buffalo, NY

Patricia Brazas
Peck El Sch
Greensboro, NC

Ann Schwabeland
Irving Park El Sch
Greensboro, NC

Bernice Perry
Brooks El Sch
Raleigh, NC

John Foley
Lewis and Clark Sch
Fargo, ND

Manna Hay
Arlington Sch
Toledo, OH

Charles Knepshield
Taft El Sch
Middletown, OH

Dawn Rowe
Brush El Sch
Grafton, OH

Ross Neidich
West Branch El Sch
Bradford, PA

Frank Rice, Jr.
Westview El Sch
Spartanburg, SC

Wilma Todd
Cooper El Sch
Garland, TX

James Goodwin
East Salem Sch
Salem, VA

Dean Rickabaugh
Highland Park Sch
Roanoke, VA

Patricia Kinner
St. Aemilian's Sch
Milwaukee, WI

Kathryn Lee
Falk El Sch
Madison, WI

Many thanks also to the principals, supervisors, and science coordinators who assisted in the arrangements for the field test.

CONTENTS

Would this picture look the same if it had been taken five minutes earlier? How different would the picture be if it had been taken one hour, one day, or six months earlier? Would you see the same clouds? Would the trees and water look the same? Would the sun be in the picture?

Everything around us seems to change. The earth is changing all the time. Some changes happen slowly. They take a long time to be noticed. Others occur in just seconds. In this unit you will learn about our changing earth.

UNIT 1

THE CHANGING EARTH

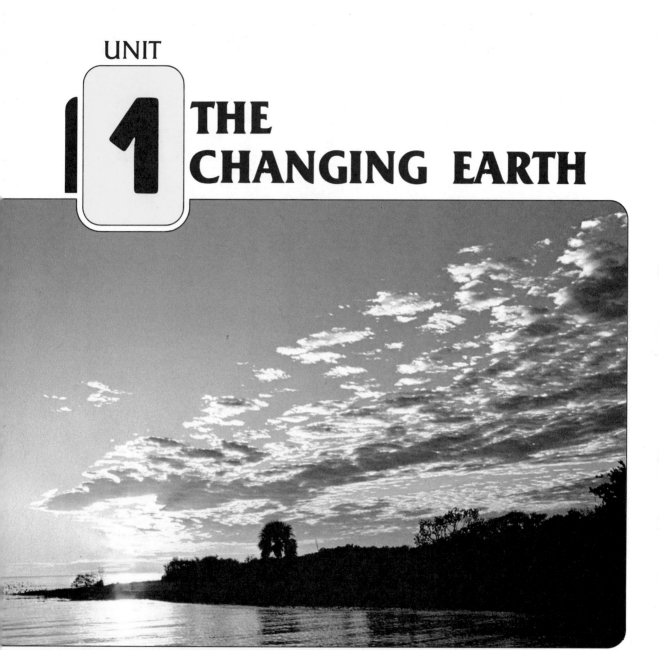

CHAPTER 1

THE WHOLE EARTH

1 INSIDE THE EARTH

Curt Brooks was a famous cave explorer. He traveled into some of the world's deepest caves, but he wanted to go even farther into the earth. He wanted to know what it was like at the center of the earth. For years he dreamed about making a machine that could take him there.

What do you think you would find if you could drill a hole to the center of the earth? Would it be very hot? What would the rocks look like?

When you finish this lesson, you should be able to:

○ Name the layers of the earth.

○ Describe what each layer of the earth is like.

If you want to know what the inside of a softball looks like, you can easily find out. You can just rip the cover off the ball and unwind all the string. Finding out what the inside of the earth is like is not as easy. We can't open the earth and look inside. We can't travel very deep into the earth. But certain clues help us make guesses about what the inside of the earth is like. You will know many of these clues when you finish this unit.

Geologists (jee-**ahl**-oh-jists) think the earth is made of three layers. The top layer of the earth is mostly solid rock and is called the **crust**.

The *crust* is very important to us. It is like a giant treasure chest. Oil, coal, gas, metals, rocks, water, and plants are some of its treasures.

If the earth were an apple, the crust would be as thin as the apple's skin. This crust (top layer) is about 4 to 7 kilometers (2 to 4 miles) thick under the oceans. It is about 35 kilometers (21 miles) thick under land. Under some mountains, the crust can be up to 70 kilometers (44 miles) deep.

Geologist: A person who studies rocks and other features of the earth.

Crust: The thin, solid, outer layer of the earth.

Mantle: A very thick layer of the earth found under the crust.

Under the crust is the layer of earth called the **mantle** (man-till). It is about 2,900 kilometers (1,800 miles) thick and is made of solid rock. If we again compare the earth to an apple, the *mantle* would be as thick as the white part under the skin. *Geologists* believe it is as hot as 3,000° Celsius (5,400° Fahrenheit) in the mantle.

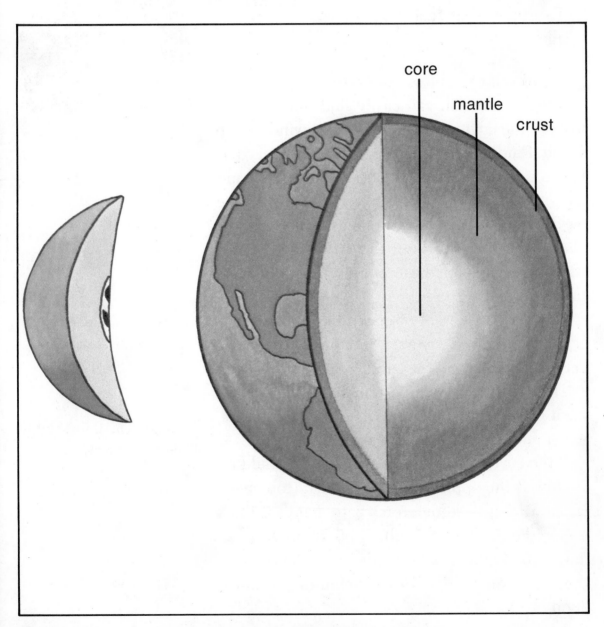

core

mantle

crust

Deep in the center of the earth is the third layer called the **core**. If we compare the earth to an apple once again, the *core* is as thick as the center, or core, of the apple. It is about 3,470 kilometers (2,100 miles) deep. Temperatures are probably as high as 4,000° Celsius (7,200° Fahrenheit) in the core. It is believed that the core is made of the metals iron and nickel.

Core: The center layer of the earth.

MAIN IDEAS

The earth is made of three layers: the crust, the mantle, and the core. The crust is the outside thinnest layer. It is mostly made of solid rock. Beneath the crust is the mantle. It is about 2,900 kilometers (1,800 miles) thick and is made of material heavier than the material found in the crust. The core is the center of the earth, and it is the heaviest layer. Geologists believe the core is made of the metals iron and nickel.

QUESTIONS

Write your answers on a sheet of paper.

1. What are the names of the three layers of the earth?
2. How would you describe each layer of the earth to the famous cave explorer Curt Brooks?
3. If you were able to travel to the center of the earth, would you? Why?

2 MOVING CONTINENTS

In 1922 a man named Alfred Wegener wrote a book about the earth. He said that the continents were joined together long ago. Then one day the continents broke apart and began moving. Most scientists did not believe him. They said it was crazy to think large pieces of land could move around on the earth. What do you think about the idea of moving continents?

When you finish this lesson, you should be able to:

○ Name the term that describes the idea of moving continents.

○ Describe how the continents have moved.

○ Name two clues that make scientists think that the continents were once joined.

ACTIVITY

Materials
construction paper
map of the world
pencil
scissors
tape
tracing paper

A. Place the tracing paper on top of the map.

B. Carefully trace the outline of North America. Write *North America* inside the tracing.

C. Repeat step B for the continents of South America, Africa, and Europe-Asia.

D. Carefully cut out the tracings.

E. Place the cutouts on a piece of construction paper. Try to fit all the continents together as you would do with pieces of a puzzle. Join South America and Africa. Above these, join North America and Europe-Asia.

F. Tape the continents in place when you finish.
    1. Were you able to fit the cutouts together?
    2. Did they fit together perfectly?

The fit of the continents is not perfect. But the shapes do fit together. This is our first clue that the continents might have moved.

Continental drift: The idea that the continents are moving.

Geologists call this movement **continental drift** (con-tin-**nen**-tal **drift**). They think that over many years the continents drifted apart at a rate of one to ten centimeters (one half inch to four inches) a year.

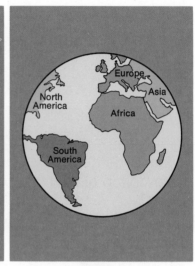

Fossils: Traces of plants and animals in rocks.

Another clue that agrees with the idea of *continental drift* comes from studying rocks. Some rocks have traces of plants and animals that lived a long time ago. These traces in the rock are called **fossils** (**foss**-sills). *Fossils* of the same kind of plant have been found on five continents. These continents are many miles apart. It is unlikely that the plants could be so alike if they came from very different parts of the earth. Geologists think that long ago, when these plants were alive, the earth was one huge continent. The plants died and left their traces on the rocks. When the continents moved apart, the rocks with the fossils moved too.

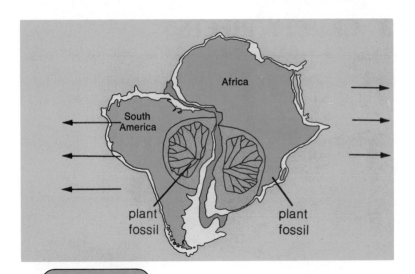

MAIN IDEAS

In this lesson you learned two clues that make geologists think the continents have moved. One is that the edges of the continents can be joined almost like pieces of a puzzle. The other clue is that fossils of the same kind of plant have been found on five different continents. The idea that the continents have moved is called continental drift.

QUESTIONS

Write your answers on a sheet of paper.
1. What is the term that describes the idea of moving continents?
2. What clues support the idea that the continents have moved?
3. Do you agree with the idea that the continents have moved?

3 CRUSTY PIECES

In the last lesson you learned that the continents appear to be drifting apart. How are such large pieces of land able to move? The ancient Hindus (**hin**-doos) believed the earth rested on the head of an elephant. The elephant was standing on the back of a tortoise. Whenever the animals moved, the earth also moved.

Today geologists have a new idea that they think explains the movements of the whole earth. When you finish this lesson, you should be able to:

○ Give the name for large sections of the earth's crust.

○ Give the name for a chain of mountains formed near the center of the oceans.

○ Describe what happens at these underwater mountains.

What happens when you turn on a radiator in a cold room? Heat from the radiator flows into the room and warms up the cold air. The heat in the earth also flows from hot places to cooler places. Hot melted rocks in the earth's mantle push their way toward the cooler crust. The hot material is able to flow through the crust at places where there are cracks. Some cracks in the crust are found along the **mid-ocean ridges** (**mid-oh**-shun **rij**-jez). The *mid-ocean ridges* are chains of mountains formed near the center of the oceans. They go around the earth and separate the crust into several large pieces. These sections of the earth's crust are called **plates** (**playts**).

On the next page is an activity that will help you understand what happens at the mid-ocean ridges.

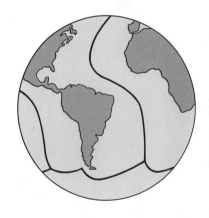

Mid-ocean ridges: Chains of mountains formed near the center of the oceans.

Plates: Large sections of the earth's crust.

ACTIVITY

Materials
cutouts of the
   continents
2 pieces of typing
   paper
2 tables
tape

A. Tape together two sheets of paper.

B. Tape the cutouts of the continents to the sheets of paper as shown.

C. Fold the paper along the taped edges. Hang the folded paper

between two tables, as shown in the drawing.

D. Place your hands on the piece of paper as shown. Spread your hands apart very slowly.
   1. How did the pieces of paper move?
   2. In which direction did the continents move?

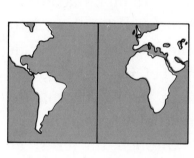

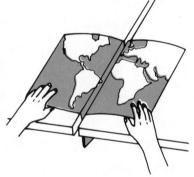

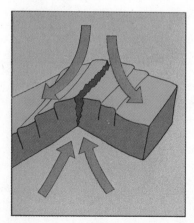

Geologists think the earth's crust moves like the paper in your activity. Hot material from inside the earth escapes through cracks at the mid-ocean ridges. It pushes up and away from the cracks like your paper moved up and away from the crack between the tables. As the hot material pushes, the sea floor spreads apart. The hot material then cools and hardens. It becomes part of the ocean floor.

12

Spreading of the sea floor is believed to be the reason why the plates of the crust move. The continents are carried along with the moving plates like they were carried along in your activity.

MAIN IDEAS

The mid-ocean ridges are chains of mountains formed near the center of the oceans. Hot material from inside the earth escapes through cracks in the mid-ocean ridges. The sea floor spreads apart as the hot material pushes up. The hot material cools, hardens, and becomes part of the ocean floor. Spreading of the sea floor moves the plates of the crust. The continents are carried along with the moving plates.

QUESTIONS

Write your answers on a sheet of paper.
1. What are large sections of the earth's crust called?
2. What are chains of mountains formed near the center of the oceans called?
3. What happens at the underwater mountain chains?

CHAPTER 2
MAKING MOUNTAINS

1 CRACKS IN THE CRUST

"It was so still and quiet outside that I could hear the birds singing. Suddenly, the table next to my bed began to rattle. Then came a thundering sound and the walls around me started to crack. All at once, the trembling stopped." What do you think caused this sudden shaking and noise?

When you finish this lesson, you should be able to:

○ Name the word that describes sudden movements in the earth.

○ Explain how cracks in the crust can cause these sudden movements.

○ Describe how moving plates may cause sudden movements in the earth.

Sudden movements in the earth are called **earthquakes** (**erth**-kwakes). During an *earthquake* the earth's crust shakes and trembles. Earthquakes happen most often in certain areas. Look at the map on this page. Each red dot shows where a large earthquake has taken place. These dots make up what is called the "earthquake belt." Each black line outlines one of the crust's plates. Do you notice any pattern?

Earthquake: A sudden movement in the earth.

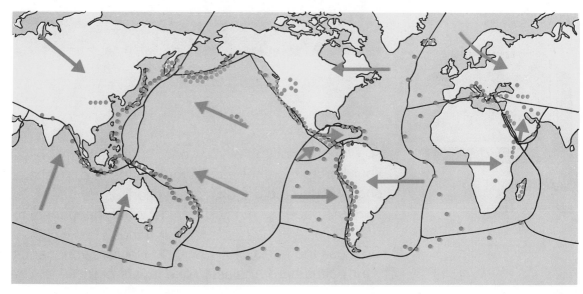

Most earthquakes occur close to where plates meet. As the plates slowly move, their edges push together. This pushing may also cause nearby rocks to move. A place where the rocks along the sides of a crack have moved is called a **fault**. Earthquakes occur along *faults*. Sometimes rocks along the sides of a fault are stuck together. Just like a stick suddenly snaps when pushed hard enough, the sides of the fault that are stuck finally slip or snap. When this happens, the earth "quakes" or trembles.

The activity below should help you understand how earthquakes happen along faults.

Fault: A place where the rocks along the sides of a crack have moved.

Materials
none

A. Place the palms of your hands together as shown in the picture on the next page.

B. Press the heels of your palms hard against each other, and move your hands in opposite directions.

1. What happened to your hands?

2. How are your hands like layers of rock?

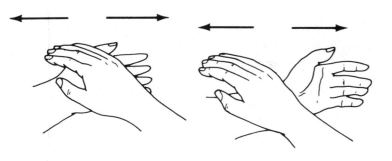

When you used a lot of force, your hands suddenly snapped and slid over one another. This quick movement is what happens during an earthquake. When enough force builds up at a fault, the rocks may quickly slide past each other.

During large earthquakes the ground cracks and buildings crumble. People can lose their lives. Geologists hope that someday they will be able to tell where and when earthquakes will take place. This will save lives and help prevent damage to property.

MAIN IDEAS

Earthquakes are sudden movements in the earth. Most earthquakes occur close to places where plates of the crust meet. A fault is a place where rocks along the sides of a crack have moved. Earthquakes are caused by sudden movements of rock at these faults. Large earthquakes can be felt for thousands of miles. They can cause loss of life and damage to property.

Write your answers on a sheet of paper.

1. What are sudden movements in the earth called?
2. Describe how rocks moving along faults can cause the earth to "quake" or tremble.
3. Look at the picture below that shows plates of the crust carrying the continents of South America and Africa. Would an earthquake most likely occur at point A, B, or C? Why?

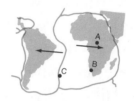

SOMETHING EXTRA

Knowing what to do during an earthquake can save your life. You and your family should know these simple rules.

1. Remain calm and alert. Do not panic.
2. If you can, move to an open field. Stay away from things that can fall, such as trees and buildings.
3. Stay away from telephone poles and other electrical wires.
4. If you are indoors and cannot move to an open field, stand under a doorway, or crawl under a desk or bed. This protects you from falling bricks and walls.

2 CONE-SHAPED MOUNTAINS

It happened on the morning of January 23, 1973 on an island near Iceland. The earth rumbled, and the ground split open. Clouds of smoke began to rise. Red-hot rocks blasted high into the air. Five thousand people ran for safety. Six months later things finally quieted down. The people returned to find part of their town buried under a cone-shaped mountain. How did this mountain get there? What was it made of? You will soon know the answers to these questions.

When you finish this lesson, you should be able to:

○ Give the two names for red-hot melted rock.

○ Name the kind of mountain formed when hot materials escape from cracks in the crust.

○ Describe where these kinds of mountains are formed.

Magma: Red-hot melted rock under the earth's surface.

Some rocks deep under the earth's surface seem to have become hot enough to melt. This red-hot melted rock is called **magma** (**mag**-ma).

Magma tends to rise toward the earth's surface because it is lighter than solid rock. The magma pushes its way out through a crack or a weak spot in the earth's crust. When magma reaches the earth's surface, it is called **lava** (lah-vah). Steam, rocks, and hot gases may be mixed with *lava*. This hot material piles up, cools, and hardens. It forms a mountain of solid rock. A mountain formed in this way is called a **volcano** (vohl-kay-no). *Volcanoes* are another clue about what the inside of the earth is like.

Look back at the map on page 15. Each blue dot shows the location of active volcanoes on the earth's surface. Active volcanoes are those that are erupting or have recently erupted. Volcanoes form a belt that we call the "ring of fire." Look carefully at the map. The ring of fire and the earthquake belt are almost in the same places. These are also the places where plates of the crust come together.

Lava: Red-hot melted rock coming out of the earth's crust.

Volcano: A mountain formed by hot materials escaping from the earth's crust.

MAIN IDEAS

Red-hot melted rock under the earth's surface is called magma. When magma rises to the surface of the earth, it is called lava. A mountain formed by hot material coming out of the earth's crust is called a volcano. Volcanoes occur in belts. They are found in almost the same places as earthquakes.

QUESTIONS

Write your answers on a sheet of paper.

1. What is the name for the kind of mountain formed when hot materials escape from cracks in the crust?

2. What are the two names for red-hot melted rock?

3. What is the "ring of fire"?

4. Look at the drawing below. Would the kind of mountain you named in question 1 most likely occur at point A, B, or C?

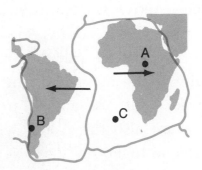

SOMETHING EXTRA

Steam escapes from the earth's surface. It only comes out where the rocks deep under the surface are partly melted. The heat from the hot, melted rocks warms up water that has seeped undergound. The heated water moves toward the surface and escapes in the form of steam.

The steam can be used as a source of power. Some cities get all their power from the steam coming out of the earth.

3 MOUNTAIN BUILDING

Look closely at this picture. It shows a fossil of a sea animal that lived a long time ago. This fossil was found in rocks that now are part of a large mountain. How did a sea animal get to the top of a mountain? When you finish this lesson, you should be able to:

○ Name three kinds of mountains.

○ Explain the way each kind of mountain is made.

You have learned that forces in the earth move rocks all the time. These forces can also raise the land and build mountains.

The activity on the next page will show you one way mountains are made.

Materials
4 sheets of different-colored paper

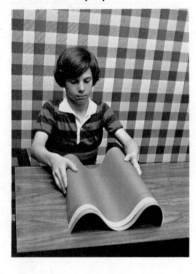

A. Lay four sheets of different-colored paper in a stack so that each color shows. Imagine that the sheets of colored paper are layers of rock.

B. Place your hands on the ends of the stack. Slowly bring your hands together.

1. What happened to the stack of paper?

Squeezing the papers caused the stack to bend or fold. Layers of rock in the earth's crust are also squeezed this way. When this happens the layers of rock may fold and lift. Mountains formed this way are called **folded mountains**. The Appalachians, in the eastern part of the United States, are *folded mountains*.

Folded mountains:
Mountains formed by the folding and lifting of rocks.

When rocks are squeezed together, they do not always bend. Sometimes they crack and tilt. When this happens, mountains are formed that have large blocks of rock separated by faults. These mountains are called **fault-block mountains**. The Sierra Nevadas, in the western part of the United States, are *fault-block mountains*.

Fault-block mountains: Mountains formed by the cracking and tilting of rocks along faults.

Dome mountains:
Mountains formed by
forces under the
surface lifting the
crust.

Magma may sometimes force its way up under the center of plates. The magma lifts the crust to form dome-shaped or **dome mountains**. The Black Hills of South Dakota are *dome mountains*.

MAIN
IDEAS

Folded mountains are formed by rocks that have been squeezed together. Fault-block mountains are formed when rocks crack and tilt. Dome mountains result from magma lifting the crust in the center of plates.

QUESTIONS

Write your answers on a sheet of paper.
1. Name three kinds of mountains.
2. How are each of these mountains formed?

CHAPTER 3

MOUNTAINS WEAR AWAY

1 SMALL CHANGES

Look at these two tombstones. They are both made of the same rock. One was placed in the cemetary in 1838, the other in 1938. They look different now, don't they? Rocks do not stay the same. They change. Most of the changes are small and happen slowly. But these changes add up. Over a very long time, entire mountains can be worn away. How does this happen? What causes these changes?

When you finish this lesson, you should be able to:

○ Name the word that describes the breaking down of rock into small pieces.

○ Identify and give an example of the two different ways rocks break down.

What would happen if you smashed a large rock with a hammer? The rock would probably break into small pieces. Nature has its own ways of hammering away at rocks and mountains. Nature's ways are called **weathering (weather-ring)**. Small pieces of broken rock are found almost everywhere we look. Just like mountain building and earthquakes, *weathering* helps to change the surface of the earth.

Look at the water pipe shown below. The pipe burst when the water inside froze. This happens because water expands when it freezes.

Weathering: The breaking of rock into small pieces.

The same thing can happen to a rock. Water drips into cracks and spaces in a rock. When the water freezes, it expands and the rocks crack and split even more. The kind of weathering is called **physical weathering** (fizz-eh-kahl). As the rock breaks down into small pieces, only its size and shape are changed. The **minerals** (min-err-als) in the rock are not changed at all.

Have you ever seen a sidewalk cracked by the roots of a tree? Plants also cause *physical weathering*. The plant roots work their way through small cracks in a rock. As the roots grow, they break the rock into smaller pieces.

There is another kind of weathering that breaks down rocks by changing the *minerals* in the rock. **Chemical weathering** (kem-eh-kahl) changes, adds to, or removes a rock's minerals. The picture on this page shows *chemical weathering*. The iron in the rock is rusting. The rusted part of the rock is a red color.

Physical weathering:
The changing of a rock's size and shape as it breaks down.

Minerals: Materials rocks are made of.

Chemical weathering: A change in the minerals of a rock as it breaks down.

You probably have seen this rusty red color on the iron parts of cars and bicycles. Rusting occurs when iron combines with oxygen and water in the air. Because it is thin and flaky, rust crumbles easily into small pieces.

MAIN IDEAS

Weathering is the breaking down of rocks into smaller pieces. The roots of plants and frozen water within rocks can break down and split rocks. This kind of weathering is called physical weathering. Only the rock's size and shape are changed. Chemical weathering acts on the minerals in the rock. Rocks that have rusted are an example of chemical weathering.

QUESTIONS

Write your answers on a sheet of paper. Look back at the picture of the tombstones on page 27 to help you answer these questions.

1. What is happening to the rocks of both tombstones?
2. Why do the tombstones look different?
3. Do you think the change in each tombstone is physical, chemical, or both? Why?

2 A DROP OF WATER

Imagine you are a drop of water. You are floating inside a cloud high in the air. Suddenly, you begin to fall to the ground. What happens to you when you hit the earth? Do you sink into the soil? Do you go back into the air? When you finish this lesson, you should be able to:

○ Name the word that describes what happens when rocks and soil are moved from one place to another.

○ Explain how the slope of the land affects the amount of rocks and soil that is moved.

○ Name two ways humans can reduce the amount of rocks and soil that are carried away.

Each day the Mississippi River carries enough broken rock to fill forty thousand railroad cars. How does the water in a river do so much work? This activity will help you find out.

ACTIVITY

Materials
glass
4 pans (2 small, 2 large)
soil
spoon
water

A. Fill each small pan with soil. Slope the soil as shown in the picture.

B. Using a spoon, make a path down the center of each pan. Place each pan within larger pans as shown in the pictures.

C. Pour two glasses of water down the path of one pan.

D. Tilt the other pan so that the end having more soil is raised 7½ cm (3in.) above the table. Pour two glasses of water down the path of this pan.

1. What happened to the soil along the sides of the path?

2. In which pan did the water travel faster?

3. If you poured more and more water into each pan, what do you think would happen?

The soil in both pans was loosened and carried away by the moving water. More soil was carried away in the tilted pan because the water flowed faster.

The paths you made in the pans were like tiny rivers. Drops of water falling on the ground may collect in real rivers. As rivers flow downhill, they carry along soil and pieces of broken rock. These small pieces of rock bang into and loosen other rocks along the sides of the rivers. **Erosion** (ee-**row**-shun) is the carrying away of rocks and soil. Rivers *erode* the land. Over a long period of time, rivers can cut very deeply into rock. Look below at the picture of the Colorado River flowing through the Grand Canyon. How do you think the Grand Canyon was formed?

Erosion: The carrying away of rocks and soil from one place to another.

We must be very careful about the erosion of our land. It takes about one thousand years for nature to replace $2\frac{1}{2}$ centimeters (1 inch) of soil. When soil is lost, it is lost for a long time. We can reduce erosion by planting grass and trees. This helps hold the soil in place. Plowing sideways across hillsides cuts down the amount of erosion. The plowed areas stop the water from flowing straight down the hill.

MAIN IDEAS

The carrying away of rocks and soil from one place to another is called erosion. Rivers erode the land by loosening and carrying soil and broken rock to different areas. Erosion can be reduced by planting trees and grass. Plowing across hillsides also cuts down on the amount of erosion.

QUESTIONS

Write your answers on a sheet of paper.
1. How was the Grand Canyon formed?
2. How does the slope of the land affect the amount of rocks and soil that is carried away?
3. Name two ways erosion can be reduced.

3 CHIPPING AWAY

A long time ago, North America and Europe were so cold that snow did not melt. Year after year, the snow piled up. This period of time was called the Ice Age. It was during the Ice Age that the snow changed much of the earth's surface. Rocks were loosened and mountains were eroded. How did this happen? When you finish this lesson, you should be able to:

○ Give the name for a large body of moving ice and snow.

○ Describe four ways that moving ice and snow cause erosion.

Glacier: A large body of moving snow and ice.

Have you ever made a snowball? What happens to the snow near the center when you press and squeeze the ball? The snow turns to ice. The same thing happened during the Ice Age. The snow near the bottom was pressed together as more and more snow piled up. Slowly the snow at the bottom turned to ice. When the body of ice and snow became heavy, it began to move. A large body of moving ice and snow is called a **glacier** (**glay**-sure). *Glaciers* flow downhill from mountains to lower ground. They erode the land by breaking rocks down and carrying them away.

Look at the picture of the mountain with the very steep sides and pointed top. This mountain was eroded by glaciers. Its rocks were pulled out by the moving ice.

Sometimes glaciers push rocks out in front of

them. Other times large rocks called boulders are carried many miles on the top of glaciers. Rocks stuck in the bottom and sides of glaciers act like claws made of steel. They scrape, scratch, and dig into the land as the glacier drags them along.

This picture activity will help you understand the different ways glaciers erode the land.

ACTIVITY

A. Look at these pictures.
   1. What happened to the rock in each picture?

   2. How do you think these things were caused?

Materials
none

Picture 1 shows scratches on a rock. The scratches were probably caused by a glacier scraping the surface. Picture 2 shows much deeper scratches. They probably were caused by a glacier pushing a large boulder. The mountain in picture 3 has only one very steep side. This mountain is in Yosemite National Park. A glacier probably plucked away much of its rock.

MAIN IDEAS

As snow piles up, the snow near the bottom is pressed together. Slowly the bottom snow turns to ice. When the snow and ice become heavy enough, they begin to move. This moving ice and snow is called a glacier. Glaciers erode the land by plucking, carrying, pushing, and scraping rocks.

QUESTIONS

Write your answers on a sheet of paper.
1. What is the name for a large body of moving ice and snow?
2. Describe four ways that moving ice and snow erode the land.

4 HUMANS CHANGE THE LAND

Look at this picture of the earth's surface. The large hole was not caused by the erosion of water, wind, or ice. Movements of the crust were not to blame either. The land was changed by humans. You are looking at a picture of one of the largest copper mines in the world. Humans have an effect on the land in many ways. When you finish this lesson, you should be able to:

○ Describe three ways humans affect the land.

○ Compare the way humans change the land to the way nature changes the land.

○ Give an example to show why it is important to know the effects that changing the land will have.

The pictures below show different ways humans have affected the land. Use these pictures to do the activity on the next page.

A. Make a chart like the one shown below.

B. Look closely at picture 1.

C. Write three things you see in the *What is happening?* column of your chart.

D. Decide whether the picture shows land being *built up, worn down,* or *not changed at all*. Write your decision in the *Land Change* column of your chart.

E. Repeat steps B, C, and D for the remaining pictures.

Materials
paper
pencil

picture	What is happening?	land change
1		
2		
3		

This activity gives you an idea of some of the ways humans affect the land. Picture 1 shows humans digging for metals, minerals, and fuels. The land is being worn down. The rocks, soil, and plant life are removed and carried away by large bulldozers, shovels, and trucks.

41

Humans also build up the land. Nature makes mountains and people make buildings, roads, and factories. Picture 3 on page 40 shows that the rocks, minerals, and soil taken from the earth are used to build things somewhere else.

Special areas have been set aside where people are not allowed to change the land. Picture 2 shows a national park. The land has not been changed by humans at all. In these areas our animals, rivers, mountains, and forests are protected.

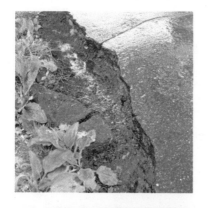

Before people change the land, they should know what effects the change will have. Think of the changes caused by building a parking lot. Parking lots stop water from seeping into the soil. Heavy rains can form rivers along the edges of these lots. The rivers carry sand and soil away. Parking lots that are built without allowing the water to drain can cause serious erosion problems.

MAIN IDEAS

Humans change the land in many ways. When we dig for rocks, minerals, and fuels, we wear down the land. When we make roads, factories, and houses, the land builds up where the soil that is removed is deposited. We can protect the land by setting aside areas where people are not allowed to make changes. Before any changes are made, we should know what effects these changes will have.

QUESTIONS

Write your answers on a sheet of paper.

1. What three ways can humans affect the land?
2. What would happen to the land in picture 1 on page 40 if a heavy rainfall occurred?
3. Describe two ways that you have changed the land.
4. How is the land being changed in the picture below?

SOMETHING EXTRA

John Muir, who lived from 1838 to 1914, was one of the first people to talk about protecting our wildlife and controlling how our land is used. These ideas are known as **conservation** (kon – ser – **vay** – shun). The president of the United States at that time was Theodore Roosevelt. President Roosevelt agreed with John Muir's idea on *conservation* and decided to protect millions of acres of forests. The conservation of our land got its start.

Today there is an area of protected forest in California called Muir Woods. It is our way of saying thanks to John Muir for helping us to remember the importance of our land.

UNIT SUMMARY

The earth has three layers: the crust, the mantle, and the core. Geologists think that forces deep inside the earth have separated the crust into several large moving plates. The continents are carried along by these plates. Mountains, volcanoes, and earthquakes are some of the effects of these movements and forces.

The earth's surface is changed by weathering and erosion. Humans also affect the land. They build it up and wear it down. We must be careful that the changes we make do not badly damage the earth.

CHECK YOURSELF

1. Match the list of mountain types on the left with the ways mountains are formed on the right.

Mountains	How formed
a. volcano	**1.** squeezing
b. folded	**2.** piling up lava
c. dome	**3.** pushing up the crust
d. block	**4.** moving the crust along a fault

2. Sudden movements of rocks along faults are called _____.

3. A rock bouncing along the bottom of a river is being
   a. heated.   **c.** protected.
   b. eroded.   **d.** erupted.

4. Physical and _____ weathering break rocks into smaller pieces.

5. Which word does not describe how a glacier erodes rocks?
   a. pulling   **c.** dissolving
   b. scraping   **d.** pushing

6. A _____ is a moving body of snow and ice.

7. More erosion occurs when
   a. the soil is covered with grass and trees.
   b. the soil has some grass and trees.
   c. the soil has no grass and trees.
   d. the soil is very old.

8. The layer of the earth beneath the crust is the _____

9. Which of the following is used to support the idea that continents have drifted?
   a. volcanoes
   b. fossils found on different continents
   c. rivers
   d. weathering

10. Scientists think the earth's crust is separated into _____

11. Digging for coal is an example of
   a. land being worn away.
   b. land being built up.
   c. land staying the same.
   d. land dissolving away.

12. Only chemical weathering causes a change in a rock's _____.

PROJECTS

1. Make an "earth mural" from drawings and pictures of land features you have learned about in this unit. The following are a few examples to help you get started: volcano, lava, fossil, folded mountain, earthquake, fault, weathered rock, glacier.

2. Think of a change you would or would not like to see in your community. Write a letter to the mayor and express your reasons for wanting or not wanting the change. Be sure to mention how the change will affect the land and people in the neighborhood.

Imagine you are in a cave like the one shown. Suddenly you cannot see a thing. What happened to the light in the cave? Where did it go?

Now make believe you are in an airplane. You look out the window and see a rainbow in the sky. You snap a picture with your camera.

Where do the colors of the rainbow come from? How do cameras make pictures? When you finish this unit, you will be able to answer these and other questions.

UNIT

2 LIGHT

 LIGHT BEAMS

1 SHADOWS AND STRAIGHT LINES

It is early in the morning on a calm summer day. You are sitting in the shade under a group of trees. You see beams of sunlight shining through the leaves.

Did you ever wonder why the sunbeams are so straight? Why do you think there are shadows on the ground?

This lesson is about light and how it behaves. When you finish this lesson, you should be able to:

○ Explain how light travels.

○ Explain how shadows are formed.

○ Tell how fast light travels.

○ Describe what happens to light as it travels away from its source.

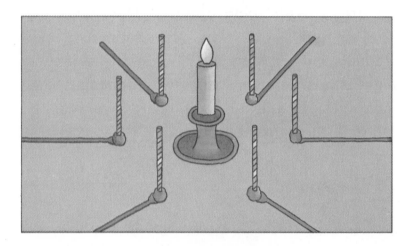

Look at the candle and the shadows in this picture. Do you think the candlelight is traveling in straight or curved lines? What would happen if the light from the candle curved around the straws? The shadows would disappear, wouldn't they? Since there are shadows, the light must be traveling in straight lines.

When objects block the path of light, shadows are formed behind those objects. If there is a space or hole in the object, the light passing through forms a straight beam.

Look again at the shadows in the picture on page 49. Every shadow points away from the candle. This tells us that light travels in all directions from its source.

Light travels very fast. It travels 300,000 kilometers (186,000 miles) in one second. Say, "three hundred thousand." In that time, a car going at the speed of light could travel around the earth eight times!

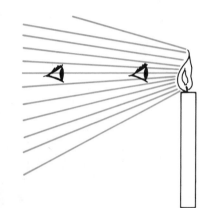

Have you ever tried to follow the path of an airplane at night? As the airplane moves away, its bright lights seem dimmer. The drawing in the margin shows why this happens. Light spreads out as it travels. When the source of light is very far away, very few light beams reach our eyes. The fewer light beams we see, the dimmer the light seems to be.

MAIN IDEAS

Light travels in all directions from its source. It travels in straight lines at a speed of 300,000 kilometers (186,000 miles) in one second. When objects block the path of light, shadows are formed behind those objects.

The further away a source of light is, the dimmer its light seems to be. This happens because light spreads out as it travels.

Write your answers on a sheet of paper.

1. What have you learned about light that is shown in the picture below?
2. How fast does light travel?
3. Why does light appear dimmer the further it is from our eyes?

SOMETHING EXTRA

How did people tell time before clocks were invented? The ancient Egyptians used a sundial. A shadow on the face of the sundial is used to tell time. A stick or marker on the dial blocks the path of the sunlight. As the sun moves across the sky, the shadow moves around the sundial. The Egyptians knew the time of day by looking at the position of the shadow. Can you think of a problem you would have if you used a sundial to tell time?

2 LIGHT STRIKES OUR EYES

Blast off! The huge spaceship roared into the sky. The crew was too busy to notice the blue sky getting darker and darker. When they finally looked out the window, they saw the bright sun in a black sky. They also saw stars.

Why were the people in the spaceship able to see stars in the daytime? Why was the sky black instead of blue? When you finish this lesson, you should be able to:

○ Give the name of the word that means the bouncing back of light.

○ Describe how we see objects that do not give off their own light.

○ Explain why beams of light are sometimes visible and sometimes are not.

A. Cut a piece of cardboard into a square. Each side should be 5 cm (2 in.) long. Use a paper punch to punch a hole in the center of the cardboard. Insert the cardboard into the slide projector.

B. Darken your room and open the door. Aim the projector across the room and out the door as shown below. Turn on the lamp.
   1. Can you see the beam of light from the projector?

C. Insert a white card into the path of light at three different places in front of the projector.
   2. Is there light each time where the card is located?

D. Walk along the path of the light and gently tap two used chalkboard erasers together.
   3. Can you see the beam of light from the projector?

Materials
paper punch
piece of cardboard
slide or filmstrip
   projector
2 used chalkboard
   erasers
white index card

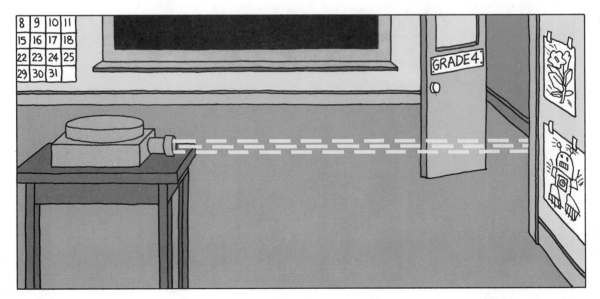

Reflection: The bouncing back of light.

You could see the light beam when the chalk-dust was in its path. The pieces of dust bounced back or **reflected** (rhee-**flek**-ted) the light to your eyes. The beam of light was hard to see before you had filled the air with the chalkdust. There was nothing in the air to reflect the light to your eyes. The white card became bright when you placed it into the path of light. The card *reflected* the light.

Before you can see an object that does not give off its own light, three things must happen. There must be a source of light. Then, the light must strike that object. Finally, the object must reflect the light to your eyes.

When a lamp is turned on, you see the bulb because it gives off light. You can see your book because it is reflecting light. But, you cannot see beams of light passing from the bulb to your book unless there is dust in the air.

During the day, dust and other things in the air scatter the sunlight. We cannot see the stars because the scattered sunlight makes the sky seem much brighter than the stars. Out in space there is nothing to reflect and scatter the sunlight. There is not any air in space. Now can you tell why the spaceship crew saw a black sky? Can you tell why the crew was able to see the stars?

MAIN IDEAS

In order to see an object that does not give off its own light: 1) There must be a source of light. 2) The light has to strike that object. 3) The object must reflect the light to your eyes. If dust or other things are in the air, you can see beams of light. The particles reflect and scatter the light.

QUESTIONS

Write your answers on a sheet of paper.
1. What is the word that means the bouncing back of light?
2. Why is the light beam visible in the picture on page 53?
3. How can we see an object that does not produce its own light?

CHAPTER 5

BOUNCING LIGHT BEAMS

1 MIRRORS AND LIGHT

Jimmy looked up to find the sun. He aimed his mirror and sent three flashes of light to his friend Carla. Carla lived in the big house on the next hill. Jimmy and Carla had a code. Three flashes meant, "I can play. Come over."

If you were Jimmy, would you know how to hold the mirror? When you finish this lesson, you should be able to:

○ Explain how mirrors change the direction of light beams.

○ Describe how you can bounce light from place to place.

○ Explain how mirrors can be used to see around corners.

A. Stand a mirror straight up and down in a lump of clay. Place the mirror and clay on a sheet of white paper.

B. Turn on the light box.

Place the mirror in the path of the light beam. Move the mirror around. Notice what happens to the light beam when it hits the mirror.

Materials
clay
lightbox
mirror
sheet of white paper
2 straws

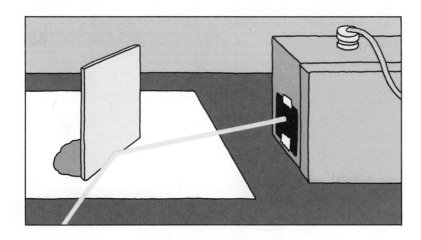

1. How can you use the mirror to change the light beam's direction?

2. How must the mirror be placed so that the light beam is reflected back onto itself?

C. Lay a straw along the path of the light beam. Turn off the light.

D. Place the mirror at the end of the straw that is facing away from the box. Turn the mirror so it forms an angle with the straw.

E. Place another straw where you think the light will reflect when the light is turned on. Turn on the light.

3. Was the second straw in the path of the reflected light beam?

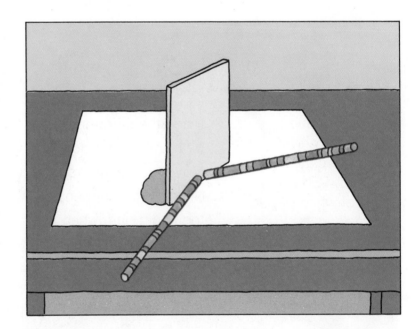

F. Repeat steps D and E until you can place the second straw exactly in the path of the reflected light beam.

G. Look at the angle the light beam makes with the mirror. Look at the angle the reflected beam makes with the mirror.

4. What do you notice about these two angles?

A mirror changes the direction of light. When you changed the position of the mirror, the direction of the bouncing light beam also changed. The light beam reflected back onto itself only when you placed the mirror head-on to the light beam. The light beam always bounces off the mirror at the same angle it hits the mirror. But it bounces in the opposite direction. When you want to reflect light to a person, you have to hold the mirror so the light bounces toward the person.

Have you ever looked through a **periscope** (**pehr**-riss-scope)? A *periscope* uses two mirrors to "see" around corners. The mirrors are placed so that one mirror reflects light beams to a second mirror. The second mirror then reflects the light beams to your eyes.

Periscope: An instrument that uses two mirrors to see around corners.

Light beams can be reflected by mirrors. Light bounces off a mirror at the same angle that it hits the mirror. To reflect light from one place to another, hold the mirror so the light bounces toward the place where you want it to go. A periscope uses two mirrors to see around corners. One mirror reflects light beams to a second mirror. The second mirror reflects the light beams to your eyes.

QUESTIONS

Write your answers on a sheet of paper.

1. Look at the diagram, below, showing a beam of light striking a mirror. Which line would be the path of the reflected light beam?

2. How does a periscope "see" around corners?

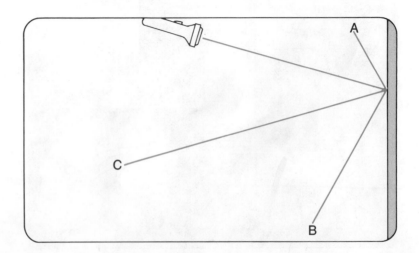

2 MIRROR REFLECTIONS

Jeannie the Great carefully dropped a silk cloth over a single light bulb. Then she waved her magic wand and lifted the cloth. There was a whole line of bulbs stretching to the back of the stage! How did Jeannie the Great do this? When you finish this lesson, you will be able to:

○ Give the name for the mirror reflection of an object.

○ Compare the mirror reflection of an object with the object itself.

When you comb your hair, you often look in a mirror. What you see in the mirror is called your **image** (im-ij). In the following activity, you will learn some things about *images*.

Image: The reflection or picture of an object formed by a mirror.

Materials
clay
paper
pencil
ruler
2 small mirrors
2 washers

A. Draw a straight line across the middle of a sheet of paper. Use clay to stand a mirror on the line. Stand the mirror up straight.

B. Put a washer on the sheet of paper about 10 cm (4 in.) in front of the mirror. Move your head until you see half the washer's image in the top edge of the mirror. Do not change the position of your head. Put another washer on the paper behind the mirror. Move the washer around until you see half of it completing the image in the mirror. Now

you can move your head.

C. Trace a circle around both washers. Take the mirror and both washers off the paper.

D. Measure the distance from one circle to the straight line across the center of the paper. Measure the distance from the other circle to the line.

1. What did you find out about the two distances?

E. Experiment with two mirrors and one washer. Try to figure out how Jeannie did her trick.

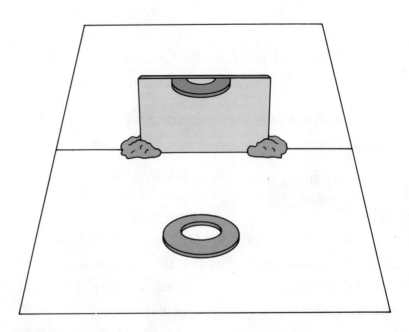

When you look in a mirror, you see an image of the things in front of the mirror. The image always seems to be behind the mirror. The object and its image always look the same distance from the mirror. Mirrors also seem to reverse images. If you stand in front of a mirror and raise your left hand, your image seems to be raising its right hand.

Jeannie the Great's trick used images. Jeannie placed two mirrors straight up and down, facing each other. She put the lightbulb halfway between the mirrors. Each mirror reflected the lightbulb. Each mirror also reflected the other mirror's reflection of the lightbulb.

This happened over and over again. The audience saw many images of one lightbulb. If you placed your two mirrors and the washer in this way, you saw many images of one washer.

MAIN IDEAS

The reflection you see when you look in a mirror is called an image. Images always seem to be located behind the mirror. The object and its image always look the same distance from the mirror. The image seems to be reversed.

QUESTIONS

Write your answers on a sheet of paper.

Have you ever seen two clowns do the mirror trick? One clown pretends an open door is a mirror. The other clown plays the mirror image. The second clown looks like the mirror's reflection of the first clown.

1. Where would the second clown have to stand if the first clown is facing the open door?
2. The first clown puts a flower in the buttonhole on the right side of her coat. What must the second clown do?
3. The first clown steps back one step. What must the second clown do?

3 CURVED MIRRORS

Beams of light swung across the top of the circus tent. They came to rest on the elephants walking in the center ring. The elephants formed a circle. They lifted their front legs and rested them on each other's backs. The beams of light from the giant spotlights moved with the elephants.

Did you know that mirrors are used in spotlights? What do you think the mirrors do? When you finish this lesson, you should be able to:

○ Name the word that means to bring light together at one spot.

○ Tell how mirrors can be used to bring light together.

○ Name three objects that use mirrors to form bright beams of light.

ACTIVITY

Materials
clay
file card (3 x 5)
lightbox
4 mirrors
white paper

A. Place a sheet of white paper about 40 cm (16 in.) from your lightbox, as shown in the picture.

B. Make a screen by bending the file card. Place it at the side of the white paper as shown.

C. Using the clay, stand a mirror in the path of the beam. Turn the mirror so the light is reflected onto the side screen (file card). Place another mirror right beside the first one. Turn it until it also reflects light onto the screen.

1. Did the light on the screen get brighter when you aimed the second mirror at it?

D. Add a third mirror beside the second one. Then put a fourth mirror beside the third one. Aim these mirrors to reflect light onto the screen.

2. What happened to the brightness of the screen each time you added another mirror?

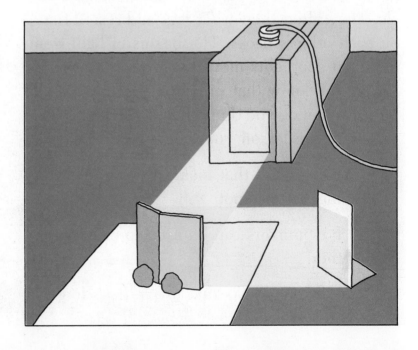

66

The mirrors gathered the light. The light was brought together on the screen. The screen got brighter each time you added reflections from another mirror. The mirrors were used to bring the light together, or to **focus** (**foe**-kuss) the light.

The four mirrors that were reflecting light onto the screen formed a curved line. Curved mirrors are used in spotlights, telescopes, flashlights, and headlights of cars. The mirrors are placed behind the bulb. They collect and *focus* the light into a bright beam.

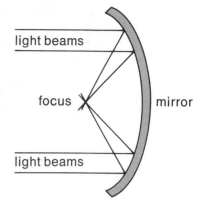

Focus: To bring together at one spot.

MAIN IDEAS

When light is focused, it is brought together in one spot. Mirrors can be used to collect and focus light. The focused light forms a very bright beam. Curved mirrors are used in flashlights, spotlights, telescopes, and car headlights.

QUESTIONS

Write your answers on a sheet of paper.

1. What is the word that means to bring light together at one spot?
2. Draw a picture that shows how a curved mirror brings light together.
3. Name three objects that use a mirror to bring light together. Tell why these objects would not be very useful without the mirror.

SOMETHING EXTRA

There is a huge solar furnace in France. Sixty-three very large mirrors reflect the sun's light and heat into the huge curved mirror you see in the picture. The heat from this furnace provides enough energy to light about 10,000 light bulbs.

Scientists think that someday large solar furnaces will be used to produce large amounts of electricity from the sun's energy.

CHAPTER 6 BENDING LIGHT BEAMS

1 LIGHT CAN BEND

Inez dove to the bottom of the pool. She looked straight up and saw something strange. She could see her friend Mark sitting on a beach chair.

How could Inez see her friend Mark by looking up at the sky? You will soon know the answer.

When you finish this lesson, you should be able to:

○ Tell what will happen to a beam of light when it passes from one kind of material into another.

○ Name the word that means the bending of light.

○ Tell what will happen to a beam of light when you change the angle at which it enters another material.

ACTIVITY

Materials
clear plastic shoebox
lightbox
milk
sheet of black paper
used chalkboard
 eraser
water

A. Place a plastic shoebox on a sheet of black paper. Fill the shoebox with water. Mix 4 or 5 drops of milk into the water.

B. Place your lightbox on one side of the shoebox. Shine the light straight at one long side of the shoebox.

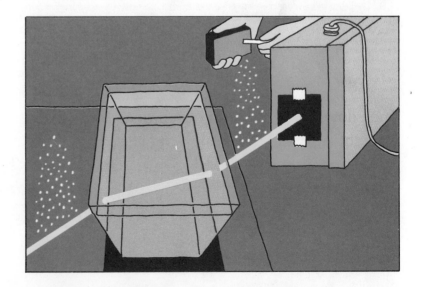

C. Scrape some chalk dust off an eraser. Sprinkle the dust into the light beam. Look down on the light beam from above.

    1. Describe the path of the light beam.

D. Move the light box so the light beam hits the shoebox at a smaller angle. Sprinkle some more chalk dust into the light beam.

    2. Describe the path of the light beam.

    3. What happens to the light beam as it goes from the air into the water?

E. Repeat the activity making the light beam hit the shoebox at a few different angles.

    4. How does changing the angle of the light beam affect the path of the light beam in the water?

    The paths of the light beam in the air and in the water were straight. The light beam bent when it entered the shoebox at an angle.

    When light passes from one material into another at an angle, it bends. The bending of light is called **refraction** (rhee-frak-shun). Light is *refracted* only as it passes into the new material.

Refraction: The bending of light.

71

Light does not bend once it is in the material. The smaller the angle at which the light beam enters, the more the light beam bends. If the light beam hits the new material head-on, it does not bend at all.

Do you know why Inez saw her friend Mark at the side of the pool? As the light coming from Mark entered the water, it was refracted to Inez's eyes. The light beam was bent a lot because it struck the water at a very small angle.

MAIN IDEAS

Light beams are refracted, or bent, when they pass from one material into another. The smaller the angle at which the light beam enters the new material, the more the light beam is bent. Light is refracted as it passes into the new material. It does not bend in the material. If light beams hit the new material head-on, they are not refracted at all.

QUESTIONS

Write your answers on a sheet of paper.
1. What happens to a beam of light as it passes from one material into another?
2. What is the bending of light called?
3. What happens to a beam of light as you change the angle that it enters the new material?

2 CURVED GLASS

Carlos and his family were on a picnic. They could not wait to eat lunch. Mom got twigs and paper to start the fire. Carlos set the picnic table. Mom said, "I can't start the fire. I forgot to bring matches." Carlos answered, "I can do it without matches." He took out his magnifying glass and soon the fire was burning.

How did Carlos start the fire? How does a magnifying glass work? When you finish this lesson, you should be able to:

○ Describe what happens to beams of light as they pass through curved glass.

○ Explain why light passing through curved glass can be dangerous.

ACTIVITY

Materials
jar of water
lightbox with 3-hole
  mask
pencil
ruler
sheet of white paper

A. Tape a sheet of white paper to your desk in front of the lightbox. Draw a straight line across the paper about 15 cm (6 in.) from the box. Turn on the light.

B. Put the jar of water on the line as shown in the picture.

1. What did the jar do to the light beams?

C. Mark the spot where the light beams come together, or focus.

74

The jar in this activity was like a **lens (lenz)**. A *lens* is a piece of curved glass or plastic that refracts light. The lens may be curved on one side and flat on the other side. It may be curved on both sides. The light is refracted as it moves from the air into the lens. The light is refracted again as it leaves the lens and enters the air. The point where light beams meet is called the focus of the lens.

Do you remember how you focused light with curved mirrors? The curved mirrors reflected the light beams to one point. A lens refracts light beams to one point. Very curved lenses bend light more than slightly curved lenses.

Where there is light, there is often heat. We all know how hot sunlight can be. When lenses focus light, they also focus the light's heat. A magnifying glass is a lens. Carlos started the fire by using his magnifying glass to focus the light and heat from the sun.

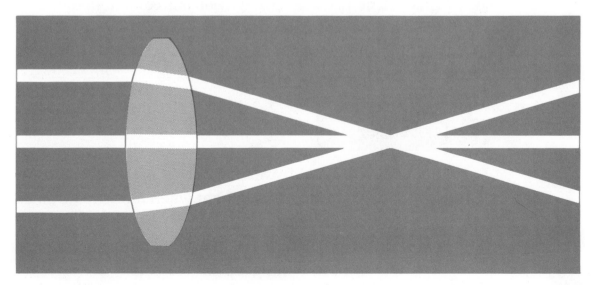

Since they focus heat, lenses can be dangerous. Never leave a lens where it can start a fire by focusing the sunlight. Don't ever look at the sun through binoculars, telescopes, or magnifying glasses. Their lenses focus too much of the sun's light and heat into your eyes. Looking at the sun through a lens for just a second can hurt your eyes.

MAIN IDEAS

A lens is a piece of curved glass that lets light pass through. Lenses can refract, or bend, light beams so that the beams come together at one place. The place where light beams come together is called the focus of the lens. Very curved lenses bend light beams more than slightly curved lenses.

QUESTIONS

Write your answers on a sheet of paper.
1. What happens to light when it passes through curved glass.
2. Why shouldn't you look at the sun through a magnifying glass or telescope?

3 LENSES FORM IMAGES

Barbara quickly brought the slide projector into the living room. She couldn't wait to see the slides of her birthday party. Dad set up the screen and pulled down the shades. Mom put the slides into the slide tray. She turned each slide upside down and left to right before placing it in the tray. Why did she do this? When you finish this lesson, you should be able to:

○ Give the name for lenses that are thicker in the middle than at the edges.

○ Describe the kind of images these lenses form.

○ Tell how a camera works.

ACTIVITY

Materials
small magnifying
  glass
white paper

A. Hold a small magnifying glass about 1 cm (½ in.) above some type in your book. Look through the glass.

1. Describe the image that you see.

B. Stand with your back toward a window in the room. Hold the white paper in one hand and the lens in the other.

C. Hold the lens about 5 cm (2½ in.) in front of the sheet of white paper. The lens should be held between the paper and the window.

D. Now move the lens back and forth until you see an image on the paper.

2. Describe the image that you see.

3. How is the image different from what you see out the window?

A lens that is thicker in the middle than at the edges is called a **convex lens** (kon – vex). A magnifying glass is a *convex lens*. A convex lens forms images by bending light beams. When a convex lens is held very close to an object, the object seems larger and right side up. In which part of the activity did this happen? When a convex lens is held further away from an object, the lens forms a smaller, upside-down and reversed image. In what part of the activity did this happen?

Barbara's slide projector has a convex lens. Now do you know why Barbara's mother placed each slide into the tray upside down and reversed?

When you formed an image on the white paper, you used all the main parts of a real camera. In a camera, the film is like the white paper. The image falls on the film instead of on the paper.

Convex lens: A lens that is thicker in the middle than at the edges.

When light hits film, chemicals in the film change. We see the image or picture when the film is developed. Film must be protected from light until you take the picture. The film is kept in a sealed box. When you "click" the shutter, a hole in the box behind the lens quickly opens. The shutter lets light through the lens to form an image on the film.

MAIN IDEAS

Convex lenses are thicker in the middle than at the edges. A convex lens forms an image by bending beams of light.

In cameras, convex lenses form images on film. The light hitting the film causes chemicals in the film to change. We see the image or picture when the film is developed.

QUESTIONS

Write your answers on a sheet of paper.

1. What is the name of the lens that is thicker in the middle than at the edges?
2. Look at the picture below. Imagine you are looking at the image formed by a convex lens. Do you think the lens was held very close to the fruit bowl to form this image? Why?
3. How does a camera work?

SOMETHING EXTRA

Your eyes have convex lenses that focus entering beams of light. These lenses form upside-down and reversed images on the back of your eye. Your brain turns the image around so that you see things right side up. Often the image formed in your eye does not focus in the right place. You get blurred vision. Eyeglasses correct your vision. An **optician** (op-**tish**-shun) is a person who makes the lenses in eyeglasses. The lens in the eyeglass and the lens in your eye work together. They bend the light beams so that they focus exactly on the back of your eye. When they focus this way, you see a clear image.

CHAPTER **7**

LIGHT BEAMS AND COLOR

1 WHITE LIGHT

Stu looked out the window to see if the rain had stopped. As he looked, he saw a wonderful sight. A rainbow had suddenly appeared in the sky.

What makes a rainbow? Why does a rainbow have so many colors?

When you finish this lesson, you should be able to:

○ Give the name for the group of colors that make up white light.

○ Name the colors that make up white light.

○ Explain how rainbows are formed.

A. Look at the light beam coming from the slide projector. Carefully follow the path of light as it goes through the glass to the screen.

1. What happened to the white light beam?

2. What colors of light came out of the other side of the glass?

3. What color light refracted most?

4. What color light refracted least?

Materials
none

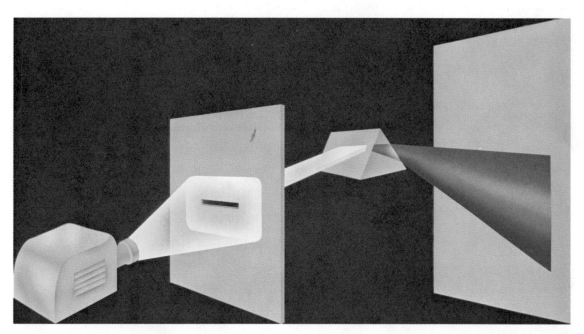

Each piece of glass in picture 1, below, is called a **prism** (**priz**-um). A *prism* breaks up white light into a group of colors called the **spectrum** (**spek**-trum). The colors of the *spectrum* are red, orange, yellow, green, blue, and violet. Prisms show us that white light is made of six colors.

Light is refracted as it leaves the prism. Each color of the spectrum is refracted a different amount. The violet light is refracted much more than the red light. Can you list the colors in order of least to most refraction?

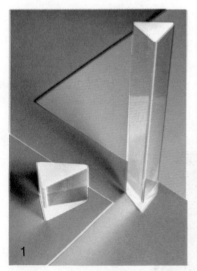

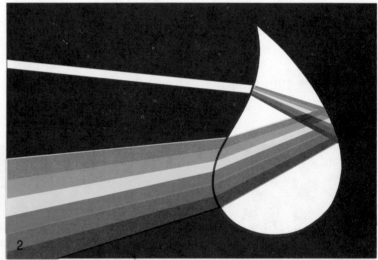

Look at the raindrop in picture 2. Sunlight first enters the front of the raindrop. It is refracted as it enters the raindrop. The sunlight reflects off the back of the raindrop and comes out the front again. The light is refracted once again as it leaves the raindrop.

The raindrop acts like a prism. When you see a rainbow, you are looking at the spectrum formed by millions of raindrops. You can only see a rainbow when the rain is falling in front of you and the sun is shining behind you. Can you tell why?

MAIN IDEAS

Prisms can separate white light into a group of colors called a spectrum. The spectrum is made up of red, orange, yellow, green, blue, and violet light. Each color of the spectrum is refracted in different amounts.

Rainbows are a special kind of spectrum. You can see a rainbow when rain is falling in front of you and sunlight is shining behind you. The raindrops refract the sunlight into a spectrum. The spectrum is then reflected to your eyes.

QUESTIONS

Write your answers on a sheet of paper.
1. What is the name for the group of colors that make up white light?
2. What are the colors that make up white light?
3. How are rainbows formed?

2 COLORS WE SEE

Lois looked at her painting. She thought the green grass wasn't quite right. It looked blue. She dipped her brush into yellow paint and added it to the grass. Her painting now looked just the way she wanted. Why did Lois add yellow to make the grass greener? Do you know why green grass looks green? Or why red paper looks red?

This lesson is about color. When you finish this lesson, you should be able to:

○ Name the word that means to take in and hold light.

○ Explain why an object is the color it is.

○ Name the primary colors.

When white light strikes an object, all the colors making up white light are also striking that object. If all the colors were reflected, the object would look white. Not all objects are white. Therefore, colored objects must be taking in some of the light that strikes them. We say that they **absorb** some light. A green object looks green because it reflects the green part of white light. It *absorbs* the other colors. A blue object looks blue because it reflects the blue part of white light and absorbs the other colors. Black objects look black because they absorb all the colors of light. Black does not reflect any light.

Absorb: To take in and hold light.

red
orange
yellow
green
blue
violet

The colors that absorb more light than other colors also absorb more heat. You probably have noticed that black or dark-colored clothes make you feel warm on a hot day. The black is absorbing the sun's light and heat. Wearing white clothes in the summer makes you feel cooler. Do you know why?

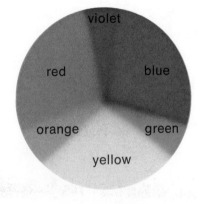

Red, yellow, and blue are called the primary colors. All colors can be made by mixing different amounts of these colors. Red and yellow paints make orange. Red and blue paints make purple. Yellow and blue paints make green. Very dark brown is made by mixing red, yellow, and blue. Artists also mix the primary colors with white to make lighter shades of each color. The artist on page 86 used the primary colors plus white to paint her picture. Now do you know why she added yellow to make the grass greener?

MAIN IDEAS

We see colors because objects reflect and absorb light. Objects reflect only their colored portions of the white light. They absorb all the other colors. White objects reflect all the colors of the spectrum. Black objects absorb all colors of light. Red, yellow, and blue are called the primary colors. Every other color can be made by mixing different amounts of these colors.

Write your answers on a sheet of paper.

1. What is the word that means to take in and hold light?
2. Look at the drawing below. What color is the ball? How do you know?
3. What are the primary colors?
4. Yellow and blue paints mixed together make:
   a. brown   b. black   c. green   d. black.

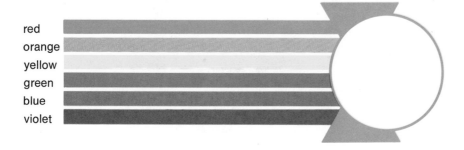

red
orange
yellow
green
blue
violet

SOMETHING EXTRA

No two stars are made of exactly the same materials. Different materials give off different colors when they are very hot. By studying the colors in a star's spectrum, scientists can find out what the stars are made of.

One tool that scientists use to study the colors of a star's spectrum is a **spectroscope** (**spek**-trow-scope). Some *spectroscopes* are made by attaching a prism to a telescope. The telescope gathers and collects light from stars. The prism separates the light into colors.

UNIT SUMMARY

Light travels in straight lines in all directions from its source. It travels at a speed of 300,000 kilometers (186,000 miles) per second. You can see light when you are looking right at its source or when it is reflected to your eye.

The direction of light can be changed by reflection and refraction. Light reflects, or bounces, when it hits a surface. When light travels from one material into another, it is refracted, or bent.

White light is made up of red, orange, yellow, green, blue, and violet light. The color of an object is the portion of white light the object reflects.

CHECK YOURSELF

1. Light travels in _____ lines.
    a. curved   **c.** straight
    b. crooked   **d.** broken

2. Light appears _____ the further it is from our eyes.
    a. brighter   **c.** larger
    b. dimmer   **d.** smaller

3. What is the word that means the bouncing back of light?

4. What is the word that means the bending of light?

5. _____ means to bring light together.

6. List three objects that use curved mirrors to bring light together.

7. Light beams bend
   a. as they pass from one material into another.
   b. after they have already passed into a new material.
   c. before they enter a new material.
   d. none of the above.

8. A _____ is a piece of curved glass or plastic that bends light.

9. What are the colors that make up white light?

10. The primary colors are yellow, blue, and _____.
    a. white   c. red
    b. black   d. green

11. What is the word that means to take in or hold light?

12. The group of colors that makes up white light is called
    a. an image.   c. a rainbow.
    b. the spectrum.   d. a periscope.

PROJECTS

1. Make a periscope like the one in your book on page 59. You will need two small pocket mirrors and a one-quart milk carton. Cut a hole 5 × 7 cm at the bottom of one side of the carton, and another at the top of the opposite side. Tape the mirrors opposite the holes at the angle shown in the picture (45° angles).

2. Use paint to experiment with the three primary colors. Mix different amounts of these paints together. See how many kinds of colors you can make.

3. Research the speeds of things such as sound and light. Find out if anything travels faster than the speed of light. Include the speed of electricity in your list.

The picture on the left shows puffy, white clouds. Do you know how they form? Do you know what kind of weather they bring?

Look at the clouds over the ocean. How are they different from the white clouds? Do they bring the same kind of weather? What kind of clouds are over your school today? Do you know what kind of weather these clouds may bring tomorrow?

This unit will help you to answer these and other questions.

3 TOMORROW'S WEATHER

CHAPTER

8

WATCHING WEATHER

1 CLOUDS

Have you ever watched the clouds and played the game "That one looks like . . . "? Do you know that the clouds and the wind help predict the weather?

When you finish this lesson, you should be able to:

○ Give the name for scientists who study the weather.

○ Identify three kinds of clouds.

Weather is the condition of the air around the earth. Clouds, rain, temperature, and wind are all parts of weather. Scientists who study the weather are called **meteorologists** (me-tee-or-**ahl**-oh-jists). *Meteorologists* help tell what kind of weather is coming.

The three main types of clouds are shown in the pictures on this page and the next. The symbol used for each cloud is shown in the lower right-hand corner of the picture.

Picture 1 shows clouds that look like feathers or curls. These clouds are found high in the sky. They are called **cirrus** (**sear**-us) clouds.

Meteorologists:
Scientists who study
the weather.

Cirrus clouds: Clouds
found high in the sky
that look like feathers
or curls.

1

Stratus clouds: Low, flat sheets of gray clouds that spread out over the sky.

Cumulus clouds: Patches of puffy, white clouds.

Precipitation: Moisture that falls from the sky.

Picture 2 shows low, flat sheets of gray clouds. These clouds spread out over the sky. They are called **stratus** (stra-tus) clouds. *Stratus* clouds turn into rain clouds as they become bigger and thicker.

Picture 3 shows patches of puffy, white clouds that look like cotton. They are called **cumulus** (**kue**-mew-lus) clouds. *Cumulus* clouds are fair weather clouds. They also become rain clouds as they get bigger and thicker.

Rain is only one kind of **precipitation** (pre-sip-eh-**tay**-shun). Moisture can also fall in the form of snow, sleet, and hail. The kind of *precipitation* that falls depends on the temperature of the air.

Clouds are carried by the wind. Wind direction is always the direction from which the wind is blowing. If a flag is blowing toward the southwest, the direction of the wind is from the northeast. Meteorologists use wind direction to help them predict the weather.

This activity will get you started on observing the weather. When you finish this unit, you will be able to fill in the whole chart.

A. Make a weather chart like the one shown below. Complete the chart so that it has a column for each day of the month. The symbols for cloud cover are shown in the margin.

B. Look at the clouds in the sky. Record the symbols for cloud type and cloud cover.

C. Use a compass and a flag to measure the wind direction. Use a thermometer to measure the temperature outside. Record both.

Materials
compass
flag
paper
pencil
thermometer (Celsius)

"Weather Record for the Month of _____"	1	2	3	4	5	6
cloud type						
cloud cover						
wind direction						
wind speed						
air pressure						
temperature						
precipitation						

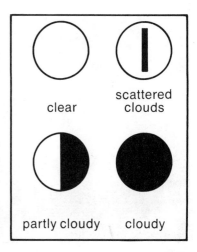

clear

scattered clouds

partly cloudy

cloudy

Scientists who study the weather are called meteorologists. Wind and clouds help predict the weather.

Cirrus clouds look like curls or feathers. Low, flat clouds are stratus clouds. Cumulus clouds are puffy, white, fair weather clouds.

QUESTIONS

Write your answers on a sheet of paper.
1. What are scientists who study the weather called?
2. Name and describe three kinds of clouds.

SOMETHING EXTRA

To most people, a meteorologist is the person on television who predicts the weather. Meteorology is more than just weather forecasting. Some meteorologists work on controlling air pollution and conserving our water resources. Others study how diseases spread. The meteorologist in the picture helps design airplanes, helicopters, and spaceships.

2 WEATHER RECORDS

Years ago people had to do their own weather predicting. They couldn't turn on the television or radio for the weather report. When farmers saw a sky like the one above, they knew from experience that they would probably have twelve hours of dry weather.

Today, meteorologists also use the word *probably* in predicting precipitation. Do you know why? When you finish this lesson, you should be able to:

○ Explain how precipitation is predicted.

○ Group weather information to look for patterns.

Weather forecasts are not always right. No one can be sure of the kind of weather coming our way. Only guesses can be made. Probably you have heard a forecast such as "70 percent chance of rain." Do you know what this means? The meteorologist has studied the weather conditions and has looked to see the kind of weather similar conditions have brought in the past. The weather records show that it rained on seven of the last ten days that have had similar conditions. So there are seven chances out of ten, or a 70 percent chance, that it will rain.

This activity will get you started using weather records to predict the weather.

Materials
pencil
thermometer
weather cards

A. Find the weather card naming the kind of cloud and wind direction you observed yesterday.

B. On the card, make a tally mark in the cloud cover column for the kind of cloud cover you observed today.

C. Make another tally mark in the box for the kind of precipitation you are having today.

D. Record another tally mark to show whether today is warmer or colder than yesterday.

E. Repeat steps A through E every day for six to ten weeks.

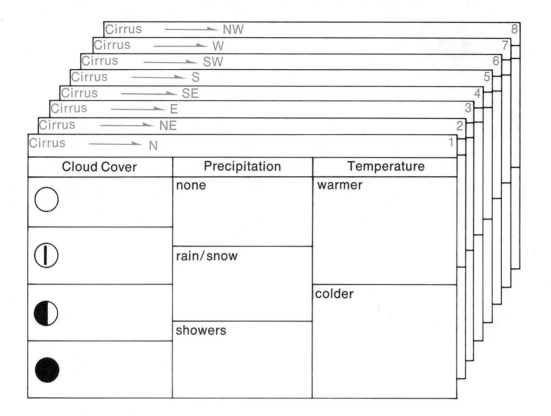

Cloud Cover	Precipitation	Temperature
◯	none	warmer
⬓	rain/snow	
◖		colder
●	showers	

After you have some tally marks on a card, you can begin using the card to predict the weather. Choose the card that matches the cloud type and wind direction for the day. Suppose today is a bright, cool day with cirrus clouds and wind from the southwest. You would look at the weather card for cirrus clouds and southwest wind. You see under precipitation eight marks for rain and two marks for none. So the chances that it will rain tomorrow would be eight out of ten or 80 percent. Suppose ten out of ten marks for cloud cover are under cloudy sky. What do you think are the chances for a cloudy day?

Weather records can be used to predict precipitation. Suppose the records show that eight times out of ten, stratus clouds are followed by rain and high winds. You can then say there is an 80 percent chance that it will rain the next time there are stratus clouds in the sky.

QUESTIONS

Write your answers on a sheet of paper. It is a spring day. The temperature is 13°C (56°F), and it is raining. The wind is from the southwest, and the clouds are stratus.

1. Look at the card shown here. What are the chances for rain the next day?

Stratus	SW	18
cloud cover	precipitation	temperature
◯		none 卌 ‖‖	warmer 卌 ‖
◐ 卌 ‖	rain/snow |	
◑		colder ‖
●		showers	

CHAPTER  9 MOVING AIR

1 AIR RISES AND FALLS

The pilot turned on the gas. Flames shot upward. The huge balloon drifted into the clouds. Do you know why the balloon rose through the air?

When you finish this lesson, you should be able to:

○ Explain what happens to air when it is heated or cooled.

○ Describe how air pressure is measured.

ACTIVITY

Materials
broomstick
chair
2 large paper bags
meterstick
paper clip
string
150-watt lamp

A. Make a balance scale like the one shown in the diagram. Bend the paperclip hook so the meterstick does not rub against the broomstick.

B. Make sure the paper bags are wide open. Hang the bags so the meterstick is level, or balanced.

C. Turn on the lamp. Hold the lamp just inside the opening of one of the bags. Keep it there until you see something change.

1. What change did you see?

2. What do you think caused this change?

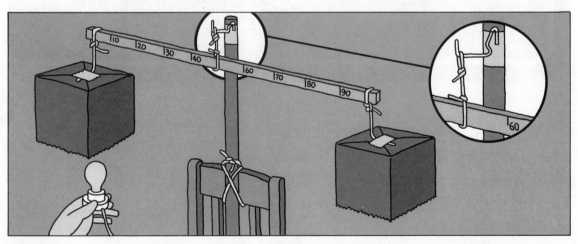

At first, the scale showed that the bags weighed the same. Then one side of the scale became lighter. The bag with the lamp under it moved up. This happened because the lamp heated the air in the paper bag. And warm air is lighter than cold air. Because warm air is lighter, it always floats up through colder air. This is why hot air balloons are able to rise. A flame heats the air inside the balloon. The heated air is lighter than the colder air around the balloon. The heated air floats upwards and lifts the balloon. What do you think happens when the air in the balloon cools?

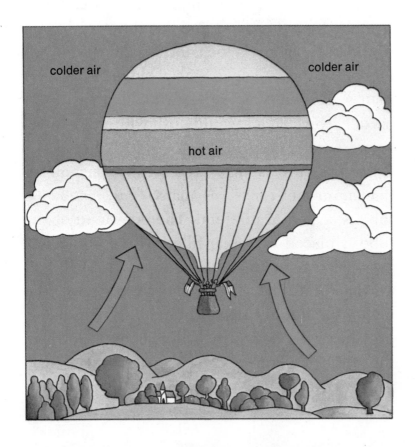

Imagine you could weigh two columns of air as shown in the drawing above. One column is cold air, and the other is warm air. If both columns stretched up to the same height, which one would be heavier? Which one would press down harder on the balance? Since cold air is heavier than warm air, the cold air would press down harder. The cold air would push with more force, or pressure.

Air pressure is measured with a **barometer** (ba-**romm**-met-err). In many *barometers,* a tube is sealed at one end. The open end of the tube is placed into a jar filled with a liquid. Air presses down on the liquid and pushes the liquid up the tube. The greater the air pressure, the higher the liquid rises in the tube. When the air pressure goes down, the liquid moves down in the tube. When air pressure changes, the weather also changes. You will learn how it changes in the next lesson.

Barometer: An instrument that measures air pressure.

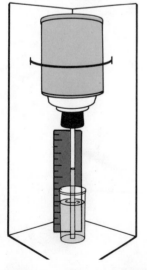

Warmer air rises through cooler air because warm air is lighter than cold air. Cool air pushes down with more force, or pressure, than warm air because it is heavier. Barometers measure the amount of pressure in the air.

QUESTIONS

Write your answers on a sheet of paper.

1. Bill measured the temperature at the three places in his room shown in the picture below. The temperatures were 18° C (64° F), 20° C (68° F), and 22° C (72° F). Which temperature do you think was recorded at A, at B, and at C? Why?

2. When the level of liquid in a barometer tube goes down, is air pressure increasing or decreasing?

2 THE WIND

Andy watched the huge blades of the windmill sweep around. He thought to himself, "I wonder what makes the wind blow to turn the windmill?"

Do you know what makes the wind blow? Do you know why the wind blows harder at some times than at other times? When you finish this lesson, you should be able to:

○ Tell what wind is.

○ Describe the direction in which the wind blows.

○ Explain what causes wind.

A. Put water in one bowl and potting soil in another. Fill both dishes to the same depth.

B. Place thermometers in both bowls. Be sure the thermometers are close to the surfaces of both. Put the bowls in sunlight.

C. Record the temperatures of the water and soil. Record the temperatures after 3 minutes, 6 minutes, 9 minutes, and 12 minutes.

1. Did the temperature of the water or the soil rise faster?

Materials
clock
paper
pencil
2 plastic bowls
potting soil
2 thermometers
water

The temperature of the soil rose faster. Soil absorbs heat faster than water. Sunlight heats up dark-colored objects quickly. Light, shiny objects reflect the sun's light and heat, so it takes longer for them to heat. Soil not only heats faster than water, but it also cools faster. This is why the land is warmer than the water on a bright day at the seashore.

Heat from the earth warms the air in the same way that heat flowing from a radiator warms up the air in a room. As the earth warms and cools, the air near the earth's surface also warms and cools. On a warm day at the seashore, the air over the land is warmer than the air over the water. The daytime air heated by the land at the seashore floats upward. The colder air over the water moves in under the warmer, rising air. This happens because cold air pushes with more pressure than warm air. Air always moves from areas of high pressure to areas of low pressure. The moving air is called a breeze or a wind. What do you think will happen at night, when the land cools faster than the water?

The greater the difference in pressure between two places, the faster the wind will blow. The chart on the next page will help you judge the speed of the wind. Mark wind speed on your weather chart each day.

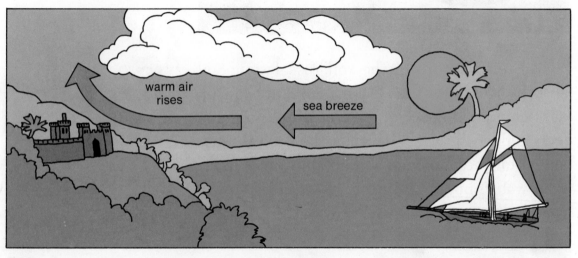

warm air rises

sea breeze

Wind Speed km/hr	Wind Class	Look For
1-11	light	leaves rustle; smoke drifts; flag moves
12-19	gentle	leaves and twigs move; light flag stands out
20-29	moderate	small branches move; dust and paper lifted
30-39	fresh	small trees sway
40-61	strong	large branches and whole trees sway; walking difficult
62-87	gale	branches broken; slight damage to buildings
89-116	whole gale	trees uprooted; widespread damage
117+	hurricane	widespread damage

MAIN IDEAS

Land heats and cools faster than water. As the earth warms and cools, the air near the earth's surface also warms and cools. Warmer air pushes with less pressure than colder air. Air always moves from areas of high pressure to areas of low pressure. The moving air is called a breeze or a wind.

QUESTIONS

Write your answers on a sheet of paper.
1. What is wind?
2. In what direction does the wind blow?
3. What causes wind to blow?

3 AIR MASSES

"And now for the six o'clock weather report. It looks like the mild weather we have had for the past week is about to end. A large, cold air mass is pushing down from Canada. The temperature will drop tonight to −25°C."

Have you ever heard a weather report like the one above? What kinds of air masses are there? When you finish this lesson, you should be able to:

○ Tell where the air masses that make our weather come from.

○ Describe the air that each air mass brings.

○ Tell where storms are formed.

Moving air at the seashore is a small example of what happens all over earth. Different places heat up and cool off at different rates. This means that the air above these places is heated and cooled differently. Warmer air is lower pressure air. Colder air is higher pressure air. As a result, large areas of high and low pressure air cover the earth.

There are six large air masses in a pushing and shoving match over North America. It is the pushing and shoving that makes our weather.

A. Look at the map below.

1. Which air masses do you think are warm? Which are cold?

2. Which are high pressure air? Which are low pressure?

3. Which air masses pick up moisture?

Materials
none

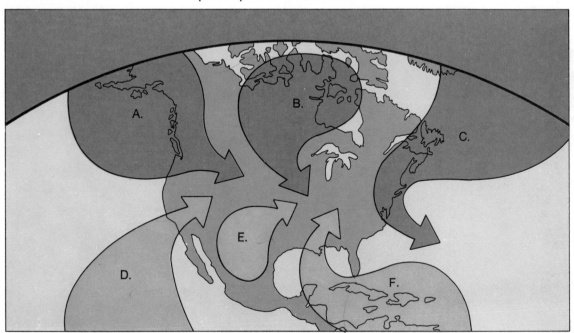

The two air masses that form over the land are dry. Dry air mass *E* is low pressure air that forms over deserts. It pushes out to the north and east, bringing clear, hot, and dry weather. Dry air mass *B* is high pressure air that forms in Canada. As it pushes down to the south and east, it carries clear, dry, and cold weather to the United States.

The four air masses (*A,C,D,F*) that move over the oceans pick up moisture. Air masses *A* and *C* bring cold, high pressure, moist air. Air masses *D* and *F* bring warm, low pressure, moist air. The moisture the air masses pick up falls as precipitation.

All places covered by the same large air mass have the same kind of weather. The temperature of these places is about the same. The amount of moisture in the air is about the same. Storms occur where air masses meet. The picture below was taken by a camera in space. Can you tell if it was sunny or cloudy where you live?

Our weather comes from six large air masses. Three cold, high pressure air masses push down from the north. Three warm, low pressure masses push up from the south. The two air masses that form over the land are dry. The four that form over the oceans are moist. Storms are formed where air masses meet.

QUESTIONS

Write your answers on a sheet of paper.

1. Where do our air masses come from?
2. What kind of air does each air mass bring?
3. Where are storms formed?

SOMETHING EXTRA

There is a wind over the United States that blows from west to east high in the sky. The wind is called the jet stream. It is almost 700 kilometers (430 miles) wide. It sometimes reaches speeds of over 400 kilometers (250 miles) per hour.

Pilots of jet planes think about the jet stream when they plan their flights. If a pilot is flying from New York to San Francisco, would the pilot want to fly in the jet stream?

10 WATER IN THE AIR

1 COLD AND WARM AIR MASSES

At 10 o'clock in the morning Sue saw cirrus clouds in the sky. At 3 o'clock that afternoon, the sky was filled with stratus clouds. Do you know what kind of weather was probably heading her way?

When you finish this lesson, you should be able to:

○ Describe how the weather changes when a cold air mass pushes a warm air mass.

○ Describe how the weather changes when a warm air mass pushes a cold air mass.

The places where cold and warm air masses meet are called **fronts**. If cold air is pushing into warm air, it is a cold *front*. But if the warm air is doing the pushing, it is a warm front.

Front: The place where cold and warm air masses meet.

Look below at the drawing of the cold front. The front edge of the cold air mass is steep. It pushes the warm air up off the ground quickly. The rising warm air cools and clouds form. Cold fronts often bring showers. Sometimes there is thunder and lightning with the shower. Usually the air behind a cold front is clear and cooler. Fair weather cumulus clouds are carried by the clear, cooler air.

cold air

warm air

The drawing below shows that a warm front is long and sloping. The warm air rides up over the cold air and pushes it away. As a warm front approaches, many kinds of clouds form. High feathery cirrus clouds are seen first. In the next 12 to 24 hours, the clouds thicken and drop lower in the sky. They change to stratus clouds and then to rain clouds. Warm fronts almost always bring rain or snow.

Drizzle: Very small drops of slowly falling rain.

Very small drops of slowly falling rain are called **drizzle** (**driz**-uhl). Dark stratus clouds bringing *drizzle* may follow a warm front. Warm fronts may take up to two days to pass. Cold fronts usually pass in a few hours.

Sometimes warm fronts surprise us. If you see cumulus clouds following cirrus clouds, the warm front is coming quickly. You may have heavy rain within 12 hours. There may even be thunder and lightning.

warm air

cold air.

The place where a warm air mass and a cold air mass meet is called a front. If the cold air is pushing into the warm air, it is a cold front. If the warm air is doing the pushing, it is a warm front.

Warm air rises over a cold front and showers often follow. Cold fronts are usually followed by clear, cooler weather.

Cirrus clouds usually form as warm fronts approach. These clouds change to stratus clouds and then rain clouds. Warm fronts almost always bring rain.

QUESTIONS

Write your answers on a sheet of paper.

1. Last night there were thunderstorms. This morning the sun is shining, the air is cool, and there are cumulus clouds in the sky. What happened during the night?

2. All day yesterday the clouds were getting thicker and lower to the ground. Was a warm or cold front approaching?

2 WEATHER MAPS

Tony picked up the paper and turned to the weather forecast. He saw a pointed line on the weather map. Do you know what a pointed line on a weather map means? When you finish this lesson, you should be able to:

○ Read a simple weather map.

○ Tell in what direction weather moves across the United States.

Weather maps use symbols to show the weather. On the top of the next page are some of the symbols used on weather maps.

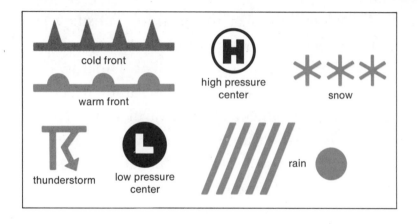

cold front

warm front

high pressure
center

snow

thunderstorm

low pressure
center

rain

The map below is a weather map for a Monday. Study this map. Then answer these questions. Over what state is the low pressure center on the map? What do the red and blue lines with the bumps and points show? If the map were printed in black and white, how could you tell the warm front from the cold front? The points on the cold front show the direction the cold front is moving. Cold air is behind the cold front. Where is the warm air? How do you know?

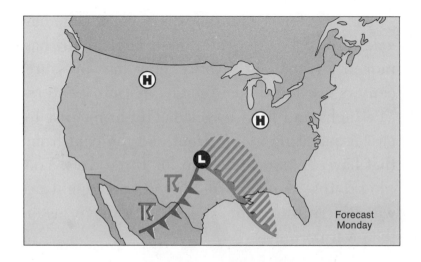

Forecast
Monday

Now look below at the map for Tuesday. You can see that the low pressure center has moved. In which direction did it move? Did the high pressure centers move in the same direction? There is rain ahead of the warm front. Notice how most of the rain is by the low pressure center. Low pressure centers are usually the centers of storms. What kind of storms are along the cold front?

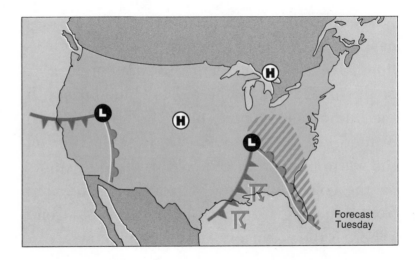

Forecast
Tuesday

The map for Wednesday on the next page has a new low pressure center on it. The old one has moved farther east. Notice how low pressure centers are followed by high pressure centers. The highs and lows travel mainly from west to east. Look at the warm front and the cold front that have been on the map for three days. You can see that the cold front has almost caught up with the warm front. Cold fronts move faster than warm fronts.

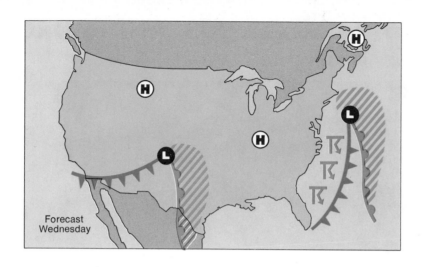

Forecast
Wednesday

MAIN IDEAS

Symbols show low and high pressure centers on weather maps. Lines with points on them show cold fronts. Lines having round bumps show warm fronts. High and low pressure centers follow each other from west to east. Low pressure centers are usually the centers of storms.

QUESTIONS

Write your answers on a sheet of paper.
Look at the weather map for Wednesday.

1. Where do you think the low pressure center above Oklahoma will go?
2. What kind of weather is Tennessee having?
3. What kind of weather will Tennessee probably have on Thursday?

3 RAIN, CLOUDS, AND MORE RAIN

José looked across the land. He saw a flat cloud just above the valley floor. "I wonder what makes clouds?" he thought. "I wonder why it rains?"

Do you know why clouds form? Or why it rains? When you finish this lesson, you should be able to:

○ Tell the name for water in the form of a gas.

○ Describe how water enters the air, forms clouds, and falls back to earth.

Have you ever wondered what happens to the water on streets after a summer rain? The water changes into a gas and goes back into the air. Water in the form of gas is called **water vapor** (**vay**-pore). This change from a liquid into a gas is called **evaporation** (ee-vap-pore-**ray**-shun). Water *evaporates* from oceans, rivers, lakes, plants, and the soil.

Water vapor is carried up by warm, rising air. When warm air rises, it cools. What do you think happens to the water vapor as it cools? This activity will help you find out.

Water vapor: Water in the form of a gas.

Evaporation: The changing of a liquid into a gas.

ACTIVITY

A. Place 10 ice cubes in a tin can half filled with water. Watch the outside of the can for a few minutes.

1. What did you see happen on the outside of the can?

Materials
10 ice cubes
tin can
water

You saw water form on the outside of the tin can. The ice cubes made the can cold. The cold can cooled the water vapor in the air near the can. The cooled water vapor changed back into liquid water.

Condensation (kahn-den-**say**-shun) is the word used to describe what happens when water vapor changes into a liquid. The water vapor *condensed* on the outside of the can.

Condensation: The change of a gas into a liquid.

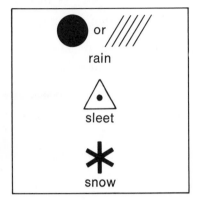

rain

sleet

snow

Water cycle: The evaporation and condensation of water over and over again.

Water vapor needs something to condense on. Clouds are formed when water vapor condenses on dust in the air. Without dust, there would not be any clouds.

As more and more water vapor condenses, the drops of water become larger and heavier. Finally they fall to the earth as precipitation. The symbols in the margin are used for the different kinds of precipitation. Use them on your daily weather chart.

What do you think happens to the water that falls as precipitation? It evaporates, condenses into clouds, and falls to the ground as precipitation again. The evaporation and condensation of water is called the **water cycle** (si - kuhl). The word *cycle* is used to describe something that happens over and over again in the same order.

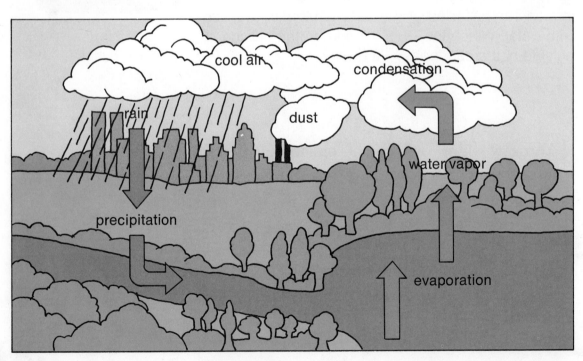

cool air
condensation
rain
dust
water vapor
precipitation
evaporation

When water evaporates, it changes into a gas called water vapor. Water vapor is cooled as it is carried up by warm, rising air. The cooling changes it back into a liquid. The vapor condenses into a cloud. Clouds bring precipitation. The evaporation and condensation of water over and over again is called the water cycle.

QUESTIONS

Write your answers on a sheet of paper.

1. Look at the picture at the bottom of page 126. Which word(s) mean *water in the form of a gas?*

2. What causes rain to fall?

SOMETHING EXTRA

Often, farmers do not have enough water to raise their crops. They hire a company to seed the clouds and make it rain. Sometimes the clouds are seeded with dry-ice. The dry-ice is dropped from airplanes into the clouds. The dry-ice cools the air and makes more water condense. Other times special chemicals are sprayed into the air. The chemicals rise up like smoke into the clouds. Water condenses on these extra things in the air and it rains.

CHAPTER 11

WEATHER AND PEOPLE

1 VIOLENT STORMS

The picture above shows a violent storm. Do you know the name of this storm? Do you know how it forms or how long it lasts? Do you know how powerful it is? This lesson is about violent weather.

When you finish this lesson, you should be able to:

○ List four kinds of violent storms.

○ Describe the kind of weather each violent storm brings.

Storms that form near the equator, over the warm oceans, are called **hurricanes** (**her**-eh-kanes). *Hurricanes* are the most powerful storms on earth. They bring heavy rains and very strong winds. They usually form between June and November. During these months, the sun above the equator is so hot that large amounts of ocean water evaporate. The warm, moist air rises quickly and condenses. A violent storm then develops.

Hurricane: A storm that forms near the equator over warm oceans.

Thunderstorm: A storm having thunder, lightning, heavy rains, and strong winds.

Storms with thunder and lightning, heavy rains, and strong winds are called **thunderstorms** (**thun**-der-storms). These violent storms often form when warm, moist air rises rapidly. Sometimes the water droplets in the clouds become charged with electricity. The electric charges jump from one cloud to another or from a cloud to the ground. We see a flash of lightning.

Tornado: A storm produced by a spinning, funnel-shaped cloud.

Powerful *thunderstorms* can produce small, violent storms called **tornadoes** (tore-**nay**-does). A *tornado* is a spinning, funnel-shaped cloud that touches the earth as it moves along. The picture on page 128 shows a tornado. Tornadoes are very powerful storms. They can destroy everything in their path.

Some storms have very cold winds and heavy snow. These storms are called **blizzards** (blizzards). *Blizzards* can be very dangerous. The freezing winds blow at a speed of over 70 kilometers (45 miles) per hour. These winds and the heavy snow make it hard for people to move.

Blizzard: A storm having very cold winds and heavy snow.

MAIN IDEAS

Hurricanes, tornadoes, blizzards, and thunderstorms, are all violent storms. Hurricanes form over warm oceans near the equator. Tornadoes occur when warm air spins up through colder air. A spinning, funnel-shaped cloud is formed. Blizzards have very cold winds and heavy snow. Thunderstorms form along cold fronts when warm, moist air rises rapidly.

QUESTIONS

Write your answers on a sheet of paper.
1. What are four kinds of violent storms?
2. What kind of weather does each violent storm bring?

2 HOT, WET AIR

It was hot! It had been hot for four days! There was no breeze. The sun beat down like a hammer. The only way to get cool was to open the fire hydrant.

How do *you* feel when the air is hot and moist? Do you feel different than when the air is cold and dry? This lesson is about the weather and how it makes you feel. When you finish this lesson, you should be able to:

○ Name the word for the amount of water vapor in the air.

○ Tell why moisture in the air can make you feel uncomfortable.

Moisture, or water vapor, in the air affects the way we feel. The amount of water vapor in the air is called **humidity** (hugh-**mid**-it-tee). On a hot summer day when the *humidity* is high the air feels sticky. The air is holding a great deal of water. When the humidity is high, you can see moisture condense on the grass at night.

Humidity: The amount of water vapor in the air.

The weather service predicts hot moist days using a *temperature-humidity index*. They call it *THI* for short. The higher the THI, the more uncomfortable you feel. Most people are uncomfortable if the THI is over 80. But if the THI is less than 70, almost everyone feels comfortable.

On hot humid days, the liquid you perspire is not easily evaporated. The air cannot hold much more moisture. This is part of the reason you feel hot and sticky. Do you know the effect evaporation has on your body? The activity on the next page will help you find out.

ACTIVITY

Materials

piece of flat
  shoelace ((3 cm)
thermometer (Celsius)
water

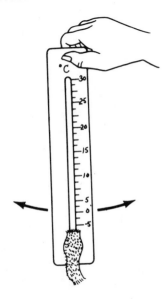

A. Take your materials outside to a place shaded from the sun.

B. Measure the temperature of the air.
   1. What is the air temperature?

C. Slip the shoelace tubing over the bulb of the thermometer. Wet the cloth with water. Gently wave the thermometer in the air for about 3 minutes.
   2. What is the temperature on the thermometer?
   3. Did evaporation make the temperature go up or down?

You saw that evaporation lowers the temperature. When the liquid you perspire evaporates, your body is cooled. On hot, humid days, evaporation is slow. Your body is not cooled as much, so you feel even warmer.

The moisture in the air is called humidity. On hot humid days, the liquid you perspire is not easily evaporated. You feel uncomfortable because your body is not being cooled.

Meteorologists sometimes report the humidity in the air with the temperature-humidity index, or THI. The higher the THI is above 70, the more uncomfortable you probably feel.

QUESTIONS

Write your answers on a sheet of paper.
1. What is the word for the amount of water vapor in the air?
2. Why do you feel uncomfortable on hot, moist days?

SOMETHING EXTRA

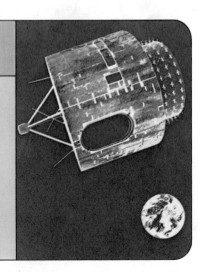

That small round ball in the picture on the right is the earth. Do you know what the other object is? It is a **weather satellite** (**sat**-uh-lite). *Weather satellites* are instruments in space. They send television pictures of the clouds to earth. Meteorologists use this information to prepare weather maps. These maps help predict the weather.

Clouds, wind, air temperature, air pressure, and precipitation are all part of weather. Meteorologists observe and measure these conditions using barometers, satellites, and other instruments. They make maps of the weather and use these maps to predict changes in weather. The maps show high and low pressure areas, warm and cold fronts, and storms. Tornadoes, hurricanes, blizzards, and thunderstorms are four kinds of violent storms. These storms sometimes do a great deal of damage.

CHECK YOURSELF

Write your answers on a sheet of paper.

1. The condition of the air around the earth is called _____ .

2. Match the name of the cloud on the left with its description on the right.

Name	Description
a. cirrus clouds	**1.** low, flat sheets of gray clouds
b. cumulus clouds	**2.** look like feathers or curls
c. stratus clouds	**3.** patches of puffy white fair weather clouds

3. Rain, snow, sleet and hail are all forms of _____.

4. A barometer is used to measure
   a. air temperature.
   b. wind speed.
   c. air pressure.
   d. wind direction

5. Warm air
   a. rises through colder air.
   b. sinks through colder air.

   c. does not move in colder air.

   d. is found high in the sky.

6. The wind blows because of

   a. different air temperatures.

   b. moving clouds.

   c. rain.

   d. storms.

7. The places where air masses meet are called _____ .

8. High and low pressure centers move across the United States mainly from

   a. east to west

   b. west to east.

   c. north to south.

   d. south to north.

9. Match the word on the left with its definition on the right.

   a. water vapor   **1.** the change from a gas into a liquid

   b. evaporation   **2.** the amount of moisture in the air

   c. humidity   **3.** water in the form of a gas

   d. condensation   **4.** the change from a liquid into a gas

10. List four kinds of violent storms.

PROJECTS

1. Climate is the average weather of a place over a period of a few years. Look up the climate of different parts of the world in an encyclopedia. Make a *climate map* using different colors to show different climates.

2. Collect pictures showing unusual weather conditions or unusual things that happened because of the weather. Try to figure out the causes or events that led up to these conditions. Make a scrapbook of the pictures.

How many machines can you name in this picture? Which ones help people to lift things? What machines move people from place to place? Do you see the wooden ladders? Are they also machines? When you finish this unit, you will be able to answer these questions.

You will be learning about machines that people use every day. Some machines are very large. Others can fit in the palm of your hand. At the end of this unit, you will even be able to invent your own machine.

4

MACHINES

CHAPTER 12 MACHINES AND WORK

1 WHAT IS WORK?

Miss William's and Mr. Green's classes are having a tug-of-war. Each side is trying to pull the other side across a line drawn on the ground. But the rope is not moving. Neither side is winning. Would it surprise you to know that these children are not doing any work?

140

When you finish this lesson, you should be able to:

○ Name the word that means a push or a pull.

○ Tell how a scientist defines work.

The students in each class are pulling on the rope very hard. They are pulling with a great deal of **force**. A *force* is a push or a pull on something. Scientists say that a force is only part of what is needed to do work. Work is done only when a push or a pull moves something. If you push on a wall, you are not doing any work because the wall is not moving. But if you push a chair and the chair moves, you are doing work.

Force: A push or a pull on something.

ACTIVITY

Materials
none

A. Look very carefully at the three pictures shown below.

1. In which pictures would a scientist say work is being done? Why?

The girl in picture 1 is not doing any work. She is holding the rock and she may get tired. But the rock is not moving. Picture 2 shows work being done. The pitcher is pushing the baseball forward toward the batter. The boy in picture 3 may think he is working hard because he is studying. But a scientist would say that the boy is not doing any work. He is holding the book, but the book is not moving.

The amount of work you do can be measured. You must know how much force you are using. You must also know how far the force has moved something.

MAIN IDEAS

A force is a push or a pull on something. Work is done when a force moves something.

QUESTIONS

Write your answers on a sheet of paper.

1. What is the word that means a push or a pull on something?
2. Shelley's new puppy Willy sees a big bone on the ground. He bends over to pick it up. Does Willy do work when he lifts the bone? Why or why not?

2 MACHINES

Even the strongest men and women cannot do all jobs by themselves. They cannot move big rocks. They are not able to clear trees from the land. They cannot do things that need a great deal of force. Ways have been found to make work easier. Have you ever found a way to help you do work? When you finish this lesson, you should be able to:

○ Tell the name for anything that makes work easier.

○ Give the name for a slanting surface sometimes called a ramp.

○ Explain how a slanting surface makes work easier.

144

Anything that people use to make work easier is called a **machine**. Perhaps when you hear the word *machine* you think of a crane or a car engine. Do you also know that many of the things you use every day are simple machines? The bottle opener in the picture below is a simple machine. When you use a tilted board to move something, you are using a simple machine. How many kinds of simple machines are there? How do machines make work easier? Let's find out!

The person loading the car is using a simple machine called an **inclined plane** (inn-**klind** plane). An *inclined plane* is a slanted surface. It is often called a ramp, a slope, or a hill. How do inclined planes make work easier? The activity on the next page will help you find out. You are going to measure force by seeing how far a rubber band will stretch.

Machine: Anything that makes work easier.

Inclined plane: A slanted surface, which is sometimes called a ramp.

145

ACTIVITY

A. Make a force measurer like the one shown in the margin. Using your ruler, mark off centimeters.

B. Pile 5 books on your desk. Tie string around a box of chalk. Attach the box of chalk to the force measurer. Lift the box straight up to the top of the book pile.

1. What was the force needed to lift the box?

C. Make an inclined plane by slanting a board from the pile of books to your desk. Use the force measurer to pull the box of chalk up the inclined plane.

   2. What was the force needed this time?

   3. Did the inclined plane increase or decrease the force needed to lift the box?

You used less force when you lifted the box using the inclined plane than when you lifted the box straight up. But you had to move the box farther. Force and distance are both used to measure work. So the inclined plane did not save you work. It just made your work easier.

People use inclined planes every day. Often they do not even realize it. Did you know that whenever you run uphill, you are using an inclined plane? Do you think you are using an inclined plane when you climb a tilted ladder? If you said yes, you are right!

Machines make work easier. They do not change the amount of work done. An inclined plane is a simple machine that has a slanted surface. Inclined planes make work easier by decreasing the force needed to move something.

QUESTIONS

Write your answers on a sheet of paper.
1. What is the name for anything that makes work easier?
2. What is the name of the simple machine often called a ramp or slope?
3. How do ramps make work easier?

SOMETHING EXTRA

This person is a **machinist** (ma-**sheen**-ist). The huge machine he is using is called a *machine tool.*

Machinists are very skilled workers. They know how to use many different machine tools to cut metal into all sizes and shapes. Their work is very important to us because many things used today have metal parts, or are made by the metal parts of machines. To become a machinist, you have to work and study with a person who is a machinist.

3 HIDDEN INCLINED PLANES

Look at this picture. There is a simple machine hidden somewhere. Can you find it? Would it help you to know that the machine is an inclined plane? This lesson is about inclined planes that do not look like inclined planes.

When you finish this lesson, you should be able to:

○ Name and describe two simple machines that are kinds of inclined planes.

○ Give two examples of each simple machine that is a kind of inclined plane.

The stairway in the picture on page 148 is a simple machine. It is a curved inclined plane. Do you recall how inclined planes make work easier? Instead of lifting something up, the inclined plane allows you to move the object along a slope. It is much easier to walk up a curved stairway than to climb straight up a ladder. You walk farther, but you use much less force.

A winding stairway is a type of simple machine called a **screw**. A *screw* is an inclined plane that winds around in a spiral. As a screw is pushed and turned into a board, its inclined plane moves through the wood. Do you think you could push a screw into a board without turning the screw? Maybe you could, but you would have to use a great deal of force.

Screw: An inclined plane that winds around in a spiral.

Imagine being small enough to walk up a screw's winding edge. Wouldn't that be like walking up a winding stairway or a winding mountain road? What other types of screws can you think of?

Another kind of inclined plane that is a simple machine is the **wedge** (**wej**). A *wedge* is two inclined planes joined together to form a sharp edge. Wedges are used to cut or break things apart. Knives and axes are wedges.

Look at the picture below. Imagine hitting the flat side of the wedge. Follow the path of the arrows. You see that your force becomes focused at the sharp edge of the wedge. Wedges focus forces to their sharp edges the way lenses focus light to one point. And it is easier to do work when your force acts only on one spot than when your force is spread out over a large surface.

Wedge: Two inclined planes joined together to form a sharp edge.

wedge—

Sometimes wedges do not look like wedges. A nail is a pointed wedge that forces wood apart. Forks and needles are also pointed wedges. Can you think of anything else that is a kind of wedge?

MAIN IDEAS

The screw and the wedge are simple machines. A screw is an inclined plane that winds around in a spiral. It is a curved inclined plane. A wedge is two inclined planes joined together to form a sharp edge.

QUESTIONS

Write your answers on a sheet of paper.
1. Name two simple machines that are kinds of inclined planes.
2. Explain why the simple machines you named in question 1 are inclined planes.
3. Give two examples of each machine you named in question 1.

4 THE LEVER

Bobby and Kim have a problem. They like to ride the seesaw, but they cannot get the seesaw to balance. Bobby weighs much more than Kim. Whenever they sit down to ride, Bobby's end goes down and Kim's end goes up. Kim always finds herself in mid air. Do you know how to solve their problem? When you finish this lesson, you should be able to:

○ Name the simple machine that has a bar resting on a turning point.

○ Explain how a bar resting on a turning point can make work easier.

○ Tell the best place to put the turning point when you want to move a heavy load.

A simple machine that has a bar resting on a turning point is called a **lever** (**lee**-ver). The bar may be a stick, a rod, or a board. A seesaw is a *lever*. The turning point of a lever is called the **fulcrum** (**ful**-krum). Can you find the *fulcrum* on the seesaw? Let's find out how levers make work easier.

The girls in the picture below are using a lever to move a heavy rock. The tree branch is the bar. The wooden box that the branch is resting on is the turning point. When the girls push down on one end of the branch, the other end moves up and lifts the rock. Suppose the girls tried to move the rock without the lever. They would need a great deal of force to move the rock. They might not be able to move the rock at all. Look what happened when they used the lever. They pushed the lever down a great distance, but used very little force. Like inclined planes, levers allow you to use less force to move things. Levers also allow you to push down to lift something up. And pushing something down is easier than pulling something up.

Lever: A bar resting on a turning point.

Fulcrum: The turning point of a lever.

A hammer is also a lever. Can you find its bar and fulcrum?

The object you are trying to move with a lever is called the load. This activity shows that when you move the fulcrum, you change the amount of force needed to move a load.

Materials
box of paper clips
flat-sided pencil
2 paper cups (small)
small box
tape
wooden ruler, 30-cm
 (12-inch)

A. Label one cup L for load. Label the other F for force.

B. Tape a cup to each end of the ruler as shown. Place a pencil on top of a small box. Balance the ruler on the pencil.

C. Put 10 paper clips into cup L. Put enough paper clips into cup F to balance the load.
 1. How many paper clips did it take to balance the load?

D. Remove all paper clips from cup F. Move the fulcrum closer to the load. Add paper clips to cup F until the load is balanced.
 2. How many paper clips did it take to balance the load?

E. Move the fulcrum closer to the load. Balance the load again.
 3. When did you use the fewest paper clips (least amount of force) to move or balance the load?

You used the fewest paper clips (the least amount of force) to balance the load when the fulcrum was closest to the load. The closer the fulcrum is to a load, the less force you need to move the load. Sometimes you can't move the fulcrum closer to the load. But you may be able to move the load closer to the fulcrum. Now do you know how Bobby and Kim can solve their seesaw problem?

MAIN IDEAS

A lever is a bar that rests on a turning point. The turning point of a lever is the fulcrum. Levers decrease the force needed to move things. The closer the fulcrum is to the load, the less force you need to move the load.

QUESTIONS

Write your answers on a sheet of paper.
1. Name the simple machine that is a bar resting on a turning point.
2. How does a bar resting on a turning point make work easier?
3. If you were lifting a pile of books, where should you place the fulcrum to make work easiest for you?

CHAPTER 13
MACHINES WITH WHEELS

1 PULLEYS

A loud groan was heard from Mr. Yen's students. Everyone was upset. The class could not see a film because a simple machine broke. Do you know what that machine was? If you're thinking that it was the movie projector, guess again!

When you finish this lesson, you should be able to:

○ Name the simple machine that is a wheel with a rope moving around it.

○ Tell how a fixed wheel and rope make work easier.

○ Tell how a movable wheel and rope make work easier.

A simple machine that is a wheel with a rope moving around it is called a **pulley** (**pull**-lee). The wheel's rounded edge usually has a groove in it. The groove stops the rope from slipping. The boy in the picture is using a *pulley* to raise the flag. He is pulling down on the rope. The rope moves around the wheel and pulls the flag up. This pulley stays in place as the load moves. The wheel is fastened to one spot. A pulley that does not move is called a **fixed pulley**.

Pulley: A simple machine that is a wheel with a rope moving around it.

Fixed pulley: A pulley that stays in place as the rope moves.

A *fixed pulley* only changes the direction of force. You pull down and the load is pulled up. The amount of force you need to lift the load is the same needed to lift it straight up. The work is easier because, as with the lever, pushing or pulling down on something is easier than pulling something up.

The pulley shown in the margin is not fastened to one spot. It is attached to the load and moves with the load. As the load is lifted, the pulley is also lifted. A pulley that moves is called a **movable pulley**. When you use a *movable pulley*, you have to pull up to lift the load. But your work is easier because you need less force to do the lifting.

Often a fixed pulley and movable pulley are used together. This makes work even easier because it changes the direction and the amount of force at the same time. You can pull down with less force to lift the same load. The cranes in the picture below have fixed and movable pulleys.

Movable pulley: A pulley that moves with the load.

The simple machine that broke in Mr. Yen's class was the fixed pulley on the window shade. The room could not be made dark enough to show a film.

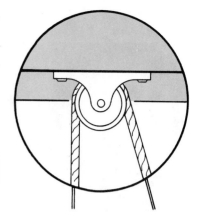

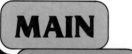

MAIN IDEAS

A pulley is a wheel with a rope moving around it. Fixed pulleys make work easier by changing the direction of force. You pull down and the load is pulled up. Movable pulleys make work easier by decreasing the force needed to lift something. Often fixed pulleys and movable pulleys are used together.

QUESTIONS

Write your answers on a sheet of paper.
1. What is the name of the simple machine that is a wheel with a rope moving around it?
2. How does a fixed wheel and rope make work easier?
3. How does a movable wheel and rope make work easier?

2 THE WHEEL AND AXLE

Opening a door that doesn't have a doorknob would be hard to do, wouldn't it? You would have to use a great deal of force to turn the rod. Do you know that a doorknob is part of a simple machine? When you finish this lesson, you should be able to:

○ Name the simple machine made of a wheel that turns on a rod.

○ Tell how wheels turning on rods make work easier.

○ Give three examples of this simple machine.

A wheel that turns on a rod is called a **wheel and axle** (ak-sell). A doorknob and the rod it is attached to is a *wheel and axle*. The doorknob is the wheel. The rod is the axle. An axle usually goes through the center of a wheel. When the wheel turns, the axle turns. When the axle turns, the wheel turns.

When you turn a doorknob, you are using force to turn the wheel part of a wheel and axle. You move your hand more than you would if you just turned the rod. But you turn with a lot less force. Your work is made easier.

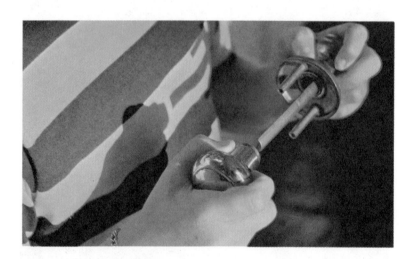

Sometimes the wheel of a wheel and axle is very hard to recognize. You can't always see the wheel. The handle of a food grinder is a type of wheel and axle that doesn't seem to have a wheel. The wheel is the circle made in the air when you turn the handle.

The activity on the next page will help you recognize wheels and axles.

Materials
none

A. Find the wheel and axle in each picture below and answer the questions.

1. Which parts are the wheels?

2. Which parts are the axles?

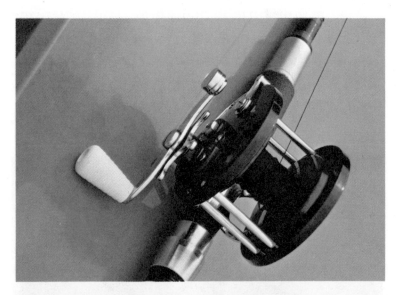

The handle you turn on a fishing pole is the wheel. The part that the handle turns is the axle. The wheel and axle on the bicycle may be a little harder to find. The wheel is the handlebar. The axle is the rod attached to the center of the handlebar. When you steer the bicycle, you move the ends of the handlebar in a circle.

MAIN IDEAS

A wheel turning on a rod or axle is another kind of simple machine. The axle usually goes through the center of the wheel. Wheels and axles allow you to use less force to turn things.

QUESTIONS

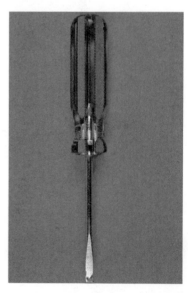

Write your answers on a sheet of paper.
1. What simple machine is a wheel turning on a rod?
2. How does a doorknob make opening a door easier?
3. Name three things that are wheels and axles.
4. Look at the screwdriver in the margin. Which part can be thought of as a wheel? Which part is an axle?

3 GEAR WHEELS

Sandra is having trouble with her bicycle. The wheels are not turning smoothly. She rode through a mud puddle and the chain became clogged with dirt. Do you know that the chain on a bicycle is connected to a simple machine? When the chain cannot turn, the simple machine cannot work. The bicycle cannot move. When you finish this lesson, you should be able to:

○ Name the simple machine that is a wheel with points, or teeth.

○ Tell how toothed wheels make work easier.

○ Explain why chains are often used to connect toothed wheels.

When you ride a bicycle you are doing work. Look carefully at the picture of the bicycle on the opposite page. The pedals are attached to a large wheel that has points, or teeth. The back wheel is attached to another toothed wheel. A wheel with teeth is called a **gear** or **gear wheel**. *Gear wheels* are usually connected to other gear wheels. On bicycles, the gears are connected by a chain. The teeth fit into open places in the chain. When you pedal, you turn the larger gear wheel. This turns the chain, which turns the smaller gear wheel. Your bicycle goes forward.

The boy in the picture is using a machine called an egg beater to mix frosting. The turning handle is attached to a larger gear wheel. The mixing blades are attached to a smaller gear wheel. The larger gear wheel turns a smaller gear wheel. In an egg beater, the gear wheels fit together without a chain. How is work made easier when larger gear wheels turn smaller gear wheels? The activity on the next page will help you find out.

Gear wheel: A simple machine that is a wheel with teeth.

Materials
crayon
egg beater

A. Put a crayon mark on one blade of an egg beater.

B. Slowly turn the large gear wheel one complete turn. Use the mark on the blade to count how many turns the blade made.

1. How many times did the blade turn?

2. Did the blade turn faster or slower than the large gear wheel?

When you turned the larger gear wheel around once, the blade turned more than once. The blade moved around more times and turned faster than the larger gear wheel. Larger gears that turn smaller gears make work easier. They increase the speed of the small gears and the number of times they turn.

Do you know a reason the gear wheels on a bicycle are connected by a chain? Look at the drawings below. The gear wheels turning without the chain move in opposite directions. The gear wheels turning with the chain move in the same direction. If the gear wheels on a bicycle were fitted together without a chain, you would have to pedal backward to go forward!

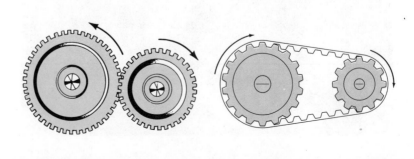

A wheel with teeth is called a gear wheel. Larger gear wheels that turn smaller gear wheels make work easier. They increase the speed of the small gears and the number of times they turn. Two gear wheels that are connected by a chain turn in the same direction.

QUESTIONS

Write your answers on a sheet of paper.

1. What is the name of a simple machine that is a wheel with points, or teeth?
2. How do toothed wheels make work easier?
3. How can two toothed wheels be made to turn in the same direction?

SOMETHING EXTRA

Most people know that Leonardo da Vinci was a great artist. He painted one of the most famous paintings ever painted—the *Mona Lisa*. Do you know that he was also a scientist and inventor? This drawing shows one of the many machines he designed over four hundred years ago. What kinds of simple machines can you find?

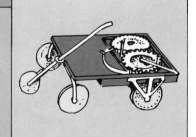

4 COMPOUND MACHINES

What would you see if you put together the puzzle shown above? Right! A bicycle! Each piece of the puzzle shows a different bicycle part. Do you notice that each puzzle piece shows a simple machine? Most machines are like the bicycle. They are made of two or more simple machines working together. When you finish this lesson, you should be able to:

○ Give the name for machines made of two or more simple machines.

○ Give three examples of things made of simple machines working together.

A machine made up of two or more simple machines is called a **compound machine** (kompound). A bicycle is a *compound machine*. The word *compound* means to mix or put together. A bicycle is made of many simple machines. The front and back wheels are wheels and axles. The handlebar and pedals are also wheels and axles. The screws that hold the seat and handlebar in place are hidden inclined planes. The toothed wheels connected by the chain are gear wheels.

The tool shown below is a compound machine called a hand drill. A hand drill is made of three simple machines. Do you know what they are? The handle of the drill is a wheel turning on an axle. When you turn the handle, you are turning a rod that moves in a circle. The tip of the drill is spiraled like a screw. It is an inclined plane. The sides of the tip are wedge-shaped. They are sharp and cut like knives.

Compound machine: A machine made of two or more simple machines.

Scissors are also compound machines. A pair of scissors is made of two levers. The fulcrum is the place where the levers are joined. Each lever also has a wedge-shaped edge used for cutting. Can you think of other examples of compound machines?

ACTIVITY

Materials
none

A. Study the drawing of the wake-me-up machine shown below. Then answer the questions.

1. What simple machines do you see?

2. How do the simple machines work together?

This is how the wake-me-up machine works. When the alarm goes off, you hit the off switch. This motion pulls a rope that is part of three pulleys. The rope pulls the board up and tilts it. The board is now an inclined plane. A ball rolls off the inclined plane and falls on a dog. The dog becomes frightened and runs. The dog's leash pulls on a peg that is holding back the string of a bow an arrow. The wedge-shaped arrow shoots and bursts a balloon full of water. The water falls right over your bed.

MAIN IDEAS

Compound machines are machines made of two or more simple machines. The word *compound* means to mix or put together. Bicycles, hand drills, and scissors are examples of compound machines.

QUESTIONS

Write your answers on a sheet of paper.
1. What is the name for machines made of two or more simple machines?
2. List two examples of the kind of machine you named in question 1.

CHAPTER  14 ENERGY

1 MACHINES AND PEOPLE

Do you know a way a merry-go-round and a doorknob are the same? They are both wheel-and-axle machines. You know how hard it is to turn the rod part of a doorknob. Imagine how hard it would be to turn the center post of a merry-go-round! Even if you could turn the post, you would get tired very quickly. We need help to run many of our machines. Where do we get this help?

172

When you finish this lesson, you should be able to:

○ Name the word that means the ability to do work.

○ Tell one important way moving water is used.

○ Name three machines that use coal, gas, and oil to run other machines.

Throughout this unit we have been talking about the force of people's muscles. You use the force of your muscles when you ride a bike, sharpen a pencil, or cut paper. But you couldn't do these things if you didn't have **energy** (en-err-jee). *Energy* is the ability to do work. You get your energy from the foods you eat. Other animals also get their energy from food. Long ago people learned that strong animals could be used to do work. Horses pulled wheel-and-axle stagecoaches. In some places oxen still pull farmers' wedge-shaped plows.

Energy: The ability to do work.

Turbine: A water wheel that uses the energy of moving water to help produce electricity.

People have also discovered that the energy in wind and water could also be used to do work. Windmills and water wheels were built. A windmill is a wheel and axle that uses the energy of the wind to run other machines. People have used windmills to pump water and grind grain. A water wheel is a wheel and axle that uses the energy of moving water. A type of water wheel called a **turbine** (**tur**-bine) supplies the energy to run a machine that produces electricity. Water *turbines* are found at large dams. These turbines are turned by the force of the fast-moving water.

Many motors are run by electricity. Electric motors are used to turn merry-go-rounds. What machines in your house need electric energy to work?

People have also discovered how to use coal, gas, and oil to run machines. The steam engine uses the steam from boiling water to run machines. Steam engines have been used to push boats and pull trains.

The gasoline engine uses the energy from burning gasoline to run machines. Gasoline engines are used to run cars, small planes, and motorboats.

The diesel engine (**dee**-zell) is a very strong engine that burns a special oil. It is used in trucks, buses, ships, and some cars.

MAIN IDEAS

Energy is the ability to do work. People first used their own energy and the energy of animals to run machines. Then the windmill and water mill were built to use the energy of wind and water. Finally the steam, gasoline, and diesel engines were invented. These engines use the energy from coal, gas, and oil to run machines.

QUESTIONS

Write your answers on a sheet of paper.
1. What word means the ability to do work?
2. Tell a way moving water is used to do work.
3. List three machines that use coal, gas, and oil to run other machines.

2 MACHINES AND ENERGY

More and more people are using more and more machines every day. Do you know you use twice as much energy as your parents did when they were your age? Machines help farmers produce food. Machines take you places and help you in school and at home. Machines even make other machines. But machines have also caused some problems. Do you know what they are? Do you know how they are being solved? When you finish this lesson, you should be able to:

○ Name two problems that machines have caused.

○ Tell a way each problem is being solved.

○ Name the word that means to save energy.

The picture on page 176 shows one problem machines have caused. When oil, gasoline, and coal are burned to run machines, smoke and gases go into the air. Some of these materials may be harmful to people, animals, and plants. The adding of harmful things to air or water is called **pollution** (po-**loo**-shun). Many machines *pollute* the air we breathe.

We are working hard to stop pollution. Factories must try to use different fuels than those that pollute the air. New cars have equipment that cuts down on the harmful gases coming from their tail pipes.

The coal, oil, and gas that provide energy to run many machines can also cause another problem. These fuels come from beneath the ground. They will not last forever. We are building new dams that use water as energy to produce electricity. But this is not enough. We need new sources of energy.

Pollution: The adding of harmful things to air or water.

Solar energy: Energy from the sun.

Some scientists feel that the sun may be the answer to all our energy problems. Energy from the sun is called **solar energy** (so-lar). The people in the house below are using *solar energy* to keep warm in the winter. The pieces of glass on the roof are called collectors. They collect the sun's heat and light. Water stored in the collectors becomes heated. The hot water is pumped into radiators throughout the house.

Conserve: To save, or not waste, energy.

You can help solve the energy problem by not wasting energy. To save, or not waste, energy is to **conserve** (kon-**serv**) energy. *Conserving* energy will help our supply of coal, gas, and oil last longer. Here are some ways you can help. Turn off lights when they are not needed. Turn off radiators in unused rooms. Fix leaky faucets. Use batteries as your source of electricity whenever you can.

Machines have caused problems. Many machines pollute the air. The fuels used to run many machines will not last forever. We are working on answers to these problems. Scientists are looking for new sources of energy. You can help by conserving energy.

QUESTIONS

Write your answers on a sheet of paper.
1. Name two problems caused by machines.
2. How are some energy problems being solved?
3. What word means to save energy?

SOMETHING EXTRA

The car in this picture does not use gasoline. It is an electric car that runs on batteries. You can recharge the batteries by plugging them into any outlet at home. Electric cars are clean, quiet, and cost very little to run. They do not pollute the air, and they help conserve our supply of gasoline. Scientists are working on ways to make these cars go greater distances before they need recharging.

Work is done when a push or a pull moves something. Machines make work easier. Either they allow you to use less force to move something, or they increase the speed and distance that the object moves. Examples of simple machines are inclined planes, levers, pulleys, screws, wedges, wheels and axles, and gear wheels. Compound machines are made up of two or more simple machines. Although machines have helped us, they have also caused some problems that we are beginning to solve.

CHECK YOURSELF

1. A push or pull on something is called a _____ .
2. A scientist would say work is being done when you are
   a. studying.
   b. holding a pencil.
   c. writing with a pencil.
   d. pushing against a wall.
3. Anything that makes work easier is called a _____ .
4. What simple machine is a ramp?
5. Name two simple machines that are kinds of inclined planes.
6. The fulcrum is the turning point of a
   a. screw.
   b. wheel.
   c. lever.
   d. inclined plane.
7. Name two kinds of pulleys.
8. A toothed wheel is called a _____ .
9. How can toothed wheels be made to move in the same direction?
10. All the following are examples of wheels and axles except
    a. handlebars.
    b. a merry-go-round.
    c. a doorknob and rod.
    d. a pair of pliers.

11. A machine made up of two or more simple machines is called a _____ machine.
12. Name three simple machines found on a bicycle.
13. The ability to do work is called _____ .
14. Tell two problems that are caused by machines.
15. Saving, or not wasting, energy is _____ energy.
16. Tell one way a problem that is caused by a machine is being solved.
17. Which of the following is an example of simple machines working together?
    a. bottle opener   **c.** hand drill
    b. nail   **d.** knife
18. A simple machine that is a wheel with a rope moving around it is a _____ .
19. Turbines are machines that use the energy of _____ .
20. What two simple machines are working together when you use a pair of scissors?

PROJECTS

1. Do some research to find out about the following machines, which were invented many years ago: spinning wheel, sickle, loom, and plowshare. You can go to the library or interview older people in your community. Find out how these machines were used, and what newer machines have improved or replaced them.
2. Cut out articles and pictures from newspapers and magazines that show problems caused by machines. Do the same for articles and pictures that show ways we are trying to solve these problems. Make a bulletin board. Use string to match or connect problems to solutions.
3. Invent your own compound machine using simple machines found at home and in school. The kitchen and the toolbox are good places to begin your search.

Animals and plants are found on every continent on earth. They are also found in the oceans.

How many plants and animals shown in this drawing have you seen before? Where do they live? Which ones no longer live on earth? You will know the answers to these questions when you finish this unit. You will learn how and why living things change. You will also find out why the different kinds of plants and animals live where they do.

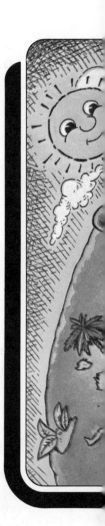

5 ANIMAL AND PLANT POPULATIONS

CHAPTER 15 LIVING THINGS

1 LOOKING FOR LIVING THINGS

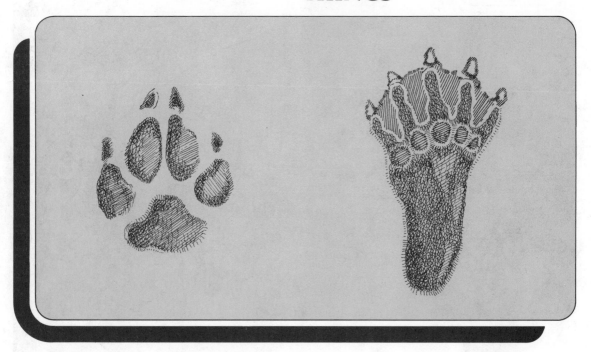

The footprints at the top of this page are animal tracks. The animals that made these tracks are shown on the next page. Can you match each animal to its footprint? In this lesson you will look for animals and plants. Sometimes you will not find the animal. You might find only a track, a seed, an egg, a nest, or a leaf.

When you finish this lesson, you should be able to:

○ Give the name for a living thing.

○ Name the word that describes a group of the same kind of living things that live in the same place.

○ Tell places to look for living things.

Plants and animals are living things. Living things can be found all around you. If you turn over a rock or an old log, you may see little animals crawling around. You can find plants growing through cracks in rocks or on the sides of buildings. A living thing is called an **organism** (**ore**-ga-niz-um). Each animal and plant shown on this page is an *organism.*

Organism: A living thing.

Organisms are rarely found alone. They live in groups with other organisms of their own kind. If you see one ant, you are sure to find many more nearby.

A group of the same kind of organisms that live in the same place is a **population** (pop-you-**lay**-shun). We belong to a group called the human *population*. In the following activity you will be searching for organisms. Your teacher will lead you on a short field trip near your school.

Population: A group of the same kind of organisms that live in the same place.

ACTIVITY

Materials
magnifying glass
notebook
pencil
stick

A. Make a chart like the one shown on the next page. Use this chart to record what you see.

B. First look at the plants. Use your magnifying glass to find animals on the plants.

C. With your stick, carefully dig into the soil. Look for animals in the soil.

1. How many kinds of organisms did you find?

2. Which kind of organism had the largest population?

3. What traces or tracks of organisms did you find?

4. What was the largest organism you found?

5. What was the smallest organism you found?

6. Are there more plants or animals where you live?

kind of organism	number seen	what it looks like

There are many kinds of animals and plants. Some organisms are very small. Others are very large. Some populations have many more organisms than other populations.

MAIN IDEAS

An organism is a living thing. Plants and animals are organisms. Groups of the same kind of plants or animals that live in the same place are called populations. In any area there are a number of populations of animals and plants. Some populations have many organisms. Others have only a few.

QUESTIONS

Write your answers on a sheet of paper.
1. What is the name for a living thing?
2. What are groups of the same kind of living things that live in the same place called?
3. Name two places where you live to look for living things.

2 COUNTING LIVING THINGS

Counting tells us the size of a population. Why do you think people want to know the number of trees in a forest, or deer in the woods, or people in a city? How are these organisms counted? Are they counted one by one?

When you finish this lesson, you should be able to:

○ Describe a method for counting a population.

○ Give an example that shows why it is important to know a population's size.

ACTIVITY

A. Copy the chart shown below in your notebook.

B. Find a grassy spot outside your classroom. Rope off an area 10 m (33 ft) on each side. Spread two bags of beans within this space.

C. Bend the wire to make a square 10 cm (4 in.) on each side. You will use the square to count the beans.

D. Drop the square on the ground over some beans. Count and record on your chart the number of beans inside your square. While counting, be careful not to move any of the beans.

E. Repeat step D four more times in different places.

F. Add the numbers in the count column to get the total count. Find the average count by dividing the total count by 5.

   1. What was the average bean count?

Materials
2 bags of lima beans
meterstick
metric ruler
notebook
pencil
rope
wire (42-cm long)

sample	bean count
1	
2	
3	
4	
5	
total	
average	

You just found the average number of beans in a 10-cm (4-in.) square. But the whole area was 10 m ((33 ft) square. It was 100 times bigger than your small square. How big is the whole bean population? To find out, multiply your average sample count by 100. By counting the population in a small space, you could figure out the population in a larger space. This is how scientists figure out population sizes.

It is important for many people to know the size of a population. Suppose someone is looking for a good place to open up a lumber company. That person would want to know the number of trees in an area. A grocer looking for a place to open up a new store would want to know the number of people in different towns. A principal has to know how many students are in school so that there are enough books and desks for everyone. Can you think of any other examples?

A sample is a small part of the whole population. We can find the size of a population by counting samples and then multiplying sample size by how many times larger the whole area is than the sample area. It is often important to know the size of a population. Principals would not know how many books and desks to order if they did not know the number of students in their schools.

QUESTIONS

Write your answers on a sheet of paper.
1. How can we figure out the size of a population without counting the organisms one by one?
2. Give an example that shows why it is important to know a population's size.

SOMETHING EXTRA

A person who studies living things is a **biologist** (bye-**ohl**-oh-jist). Some *biologists* are interested in knowing how animals live. Others want to learn more about how plants live. Biologists spend much of their time watching living things in their homes.

CHAPTER 16 THE SIZE OF POPULATIONS

1 WAYS ANIMALS REPRODUCE

Baby salmon are born in a stream. Soon after their birth they swim downstream into the ocean. They live in the ocean most of their lives. These salmon are returning to their birthplace to lay eggs. Salmon only lay their eggs in the stream in which they were born. Somehow they are able to find their way back.

When you finish this lesson, you should be able to:

○ Explain why birth is important to a population.

○ Describe some ways animals are born.

Below is an enlarged picture of a very small animal that is about the size of a comma. This animal lives in salt water. It is a picture of a **brine shrimp.** The little dark dots next to the animal are *brine shrimp* eggs. The eggs are very tiny. Brine shrimp **reproduce** (rhee-pro-**doos**) by laying eggs. When the eggs hatch, the population changes size because new shrimp are added. The birth of animals helps populations grow and survive. What do you think would happen to the brine shrimp population if the shrimp stopped laying eggs?

Brine shrimp:
A very small animal that lives in salt water.

Reproduce:
To make more of the same kind of organism.

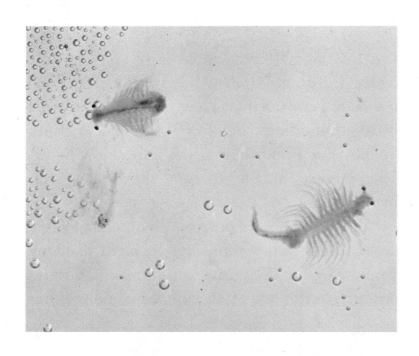

Let's see how another population *reproduces*.
Picture 1 below shows a very tiny animal found
in pond water. The animal is called an **amoeba**
(ah-**mee**-bah). An *amoeba* does not hatch from
an egg. The amoeba population grows in a
different way. Each amoeba reproduces itself
by dividing in half. Pictures 2 and 3 show how
an amoeba does this.

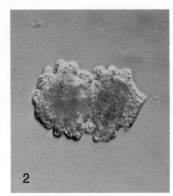
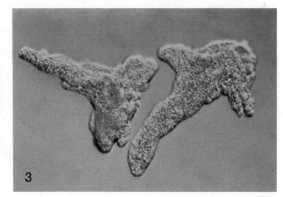

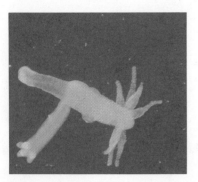

A tiny animal found in lakes and ponds is the
hydra (**hi**-drah). *Hydras* live on the stems and
leaves of water plants. They reproduce by what
is called budding. They form little buds on their
bodies. Each bud then grows into a new hydra.
The picture in the margin shows how this
happens.

Not all animals are born by dividing, hatching,
or budding. Many animals give birth to living
young, Horses, dogs, cats, and human beings reproduce in this way. Can you think of any other
organisms?

MAIN IDEAS

Animal populations reproduce in different ways. Some animals divide in half. Some lay eggs. Others reproduce by budding. Many animals give birth to living young.

QUESTIONS

Write your answers on a sheet of paper.
1. Why is birth important to a population?
2. What are three different ways that animals are born?

195

The bee in this picture is looking for food. The bee doesn't know it, but it is helping the flower make more plants. How does the bee do this? How are new plants made? When you finish this lesson, you should be able to:

○ Describe how flowering plants reproduce.

○ Tell how plants reproduce without seeds.

Many plants have flowers. The flowers usually grow in the spring. Look at the flower shown below. One part of the flower is called the **anther** (**an**-thur). *Anthers* make a yellowish powder called **pollen** (**pahl**-len). Another part of every flower is called the **stigma** (**stig**-mah). Before a flower can begin making a new plant, the *pollen* must travel from the anther to the *stigma*. This is how bees and other insects help. When insects walk on flowers, they often catch pollen on their bodies. They carry the pollen from the anthers to the stigmas. Wind, water, birds, and other animals also carry pollen. Once pollen reaches a stigma, we say that the flower is pollinated. Soon after this happens, seeds begin to grow. Most new plants grow from seeds.

Anther: A part of a flower.

Pollen: A yellowish powder made by the anthers of a flower.

Stigma: A part of a flower.

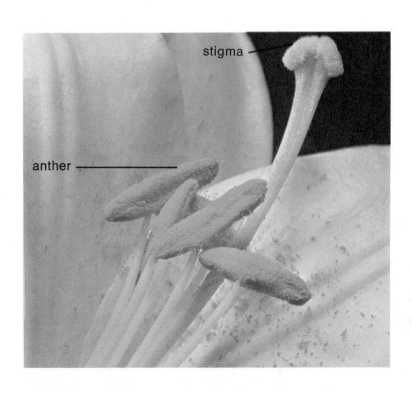

stigma

anther

Fruit trees are flowering plants. The fruits grow around the seeds. Often fruits fall to the ground and dry up. But their seeds stay in the soil and can begin to grow into new fruit trees. In a few years the new trees will flower, and pollination starts all over again. The new trees add to the size of the fruit tree population. The reproduction of plants is necessary if a plant population is to survive.

Some plants can reproduce without seeds. They can grow if you plant pieces from their roots, stems, or leaves. Potatoes grow tiny buds called eyes. If you plant a piece of potato, the eyes will grow into a potato plant.

Strawberries can reproduce by runners. A runner is a stem that has buds. When the bud touches the ground, it will grow into a new plant.

Flowering plants reproduce when pollen travels from the flower's anther to its stigma. Soon after pollination, seeds begin to grow. Most new plants grow from seeds. Some plants can grow from cuttings, buds, and runners.

QUESTIONS

Write your answers on a sheet of paper.
1. How do flowering plants reproduce?
2. What are two ways that a plant can reproduce without seeds?

SOMETHING EXTRA

Luther Burbank spent his whole life working and experimenting with plants. He is most famous for making a **plumcot** (**plum**-kaht) and a **pomato** (poe-**may**-toe). A *plumcot* is a fruit that is part plum and part apricot. A *pomato* is part tomato and part potato. Pomatoes look like small tomatoes, but they grow on potato vines. Luther Burbank also made the white blackberry. You can look through this fruit and see the seeds inside the berry.

3 POPULATION EXPLOSIONS

Have you ever been to a beach that was so crowded you couldn't find a place to put your blanket? Sometimes there are too many members of the same population living in one place. Why do you think this happens? What problems can this cause?

When you finish this lesson, you should be able to:

○ Name the term that means the fast growth of a population.

○ Tell four things that change a population's size.

○ Tell what problems can occur if a population gets too large.

Some people think there are too many people living in the world today. They say that our population is increasing too quickly. The following activity will show you how the human population has grown.

Materials
none

A. Study the graph below.

1. How many people were living in the year 1?

2. How many years did it take the human population to double from the year 1?

3. When did the population reach 1 billion people?

4. How many years passed before the population doubled from 1 billion to 2 billion? from 2 billion to 4 billion?

5. What has been happening to the amount of time it takes our population to double itself?

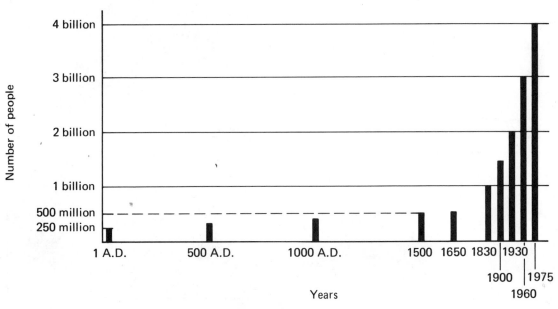

The graph shows there were 250 million people living on the earth in the year 1. In the year 1500, the human population doubled itself to 500 million. By 1830 our population reached 1 billion people. One hundred years later the number of people doubled to 2 billion. And just 45 years later, our population reached 4 billion. Our population has been taking less and less time to double itself. In only 150 years it has grown over four times as big. Many people call this rapid growth the **population explosion** (ex-**splo**-shun).

Populations increase if there are more births than deaths. They also increase if more of their members move into the area. Populations decrease if more deaths occur than births. They also decrease if their members move out of the area.

Population explosion: The rapid growth of a population.

Births

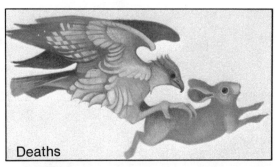
Deaths

Moving into a Place

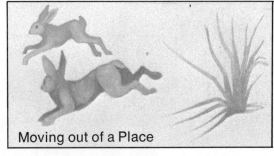
Moving out of a Place

Population explosions can cause many problems. Food supplies become low. Organisms can starve to death. Living space becomes crowded. Members of the population fight for this space. Disease spreads faster because organisms are so close to each other. These problems are causing human beings to think about the increasing size of their population.

MAIN IDEAS

The fast growth of a population is called a population explosion. A population's size depends on births, deaths, and the movement of its members in and out of an area. Problems can occur if populations become too large.

QUESTIONS

Write your answers on a sheet of paper.
1. What term means the fast growth of a population?
2. What four things control a population's size?
3. What problems can occur if a population becomes too large?

17 SURVIVAL AND CHANGE

1 ANIMAL HOMES

Each year many animals travel to new homes when the seasons change. Some animals journey more than 16,000 kilometers (10,000 miles) across two continents. Others have been sighted at heights of 6,000 meters (20,000 feet). Why do you think they do this each year?

When you finish this lesson, you should be able to:

○ Name the word that means everything in the surroundings that affects an organism's life.

○ Tell why two different animals live where they do.

○ Explain why animals move to new surroundings.

Everything in the surroundings that affects an organism's life is that organism's **environment** (en-**vie**-ruhn-ment). Living things get what they need from their *environment*. They live in places best suited to their needs.

Camels, for example, are able to store water in their bodies. The also use very little water

Environment: Everything in the surroundings that affects an organism's life.

each day. They can live in the dry desert. **Caribou** (**care**-eh-boo) are a kind of deer found in very cold places. *Caribou* do not need a warm environment to survive because their thick fur protects them from the cold.

Rabbits and deer make their home in forests. These animals are plant eaters. They need an environment where there are lots of trees, shrubs, and other plants.

Often environments change and animals are no longer able to get the things they need. When this happens, many animals move to new homes. The movement of animals from one place to another is called **migration** (my-**gray**-shun). Many groups of animals *migrate* each year.

Some bird populations migrate to new feeding grounds. Others are not able to survive cold weather. They fly south in winter to live in warmer places. Many animals move down from the mountains to the lower ground where it is warmer. Whatever the reason, animals migrate to get the things they need to survive.

MAIN IDEAS

An organism's environment is everything in the surroundings that affects its life. Animals live in those places best suited to their needs. Migration occurs when living things are not able to get the things they need from their environment.

QUESTIONS

Write your answers on a sheet of paper.

1. What is the word that means everything in the surroundings that affects an organism's life?

2. Tell why any two of the following animals live where they do.

rabbits	deer
camels	caribou

3. Why do animals migrate to new environments?

2 PLANT HOMES

Some people know just how to take care of plants. We sometimes say these people have a "green thumb." Do you know what plants need to help them grow? When you finish this lesson, you should be able to:

○ Name four things plants need to grow.

○ Tell why plants grow differently in different environments.

Plants need soil, water, light, and the right temperature to grow. Like animals, plants get these things from their environments. Do all plants need the same amounts of the same things? This activity will help you find out.

A. Make a chart like the one shown below.

B. Your teacher will show you four plants — two at a time. Describe each plant by filling in the columns on the chart.

   1. How are the first two plants different?

   2. How are the second two plants different?

   3. What kind of environment do you think each of the four plants grew in? Choose from environments A, B, or C below:

   A. no light, moist soil, room temperature

   B. light, moist soil, room temperature

   C. light, dry soil, room temperature

Materials
paper
pencil

	1	2	Plant 3	4
soil (moist or dry)				
color of the plant				
height of the plant				
stem (stiff or wilted)				

You saw that the same kind of plant grows differently in different environments. The plant that grew in the light looked much healthier.

Some plants need much more light than others. Green plants need a great deal of light. They grow best in places where there is plenty of sunshine.

You also saw that the plant that grew in the moist environment was healthier looking. It was taller. Its leaves were green. Some plants grow better in wet places where there is plenty of rainfall. Other plants, like the **cactus** (kak-tuss), do not need much water at all. A *cactus* can grow in deserts and other dry places.

Cactus: A plant that does not need much water.

Soil gives plants the water and food they need. Plants also grow differently in different kinds of soil. Some plants grow best in dry, sandy soil. Others must have moist soil.

The temperature of the air also affects plants. The picture on the next page shows the tree line on the side of a mountain. The trees will not grow any higher because the temperatures are too cold for too much of the year.

MAIN IDEAS

Plants need soil, water, light, and the right temperature to grow. They get these things from their environments. Plants grow differently in different environments because not all plants need the same amounts of the same things.

QUESTIONS

Write your answers on a sheet of paper.

1. What are the four things plants need from their environments?

2. Mary bought two different plants and put them on the same windowsill. She made sure that both plants received the same amount of water and sunshine. Each plant's soil was also the same. Why did one plant grow much better than the other?

3 MEASURING LIVING THINGS

There are many sizes of plants and animals. Even the same kind of living things differ in size. Does an organism's size have anything to do with helping it survive? When you finish this lesson, you should be able to:

○ Find the average size of a population.

○ Tell how one organism's size has helped it survive.

How tall are you? How tall are your classmates? What is the average height of the people in your class? You will need a partner to find out.

A. Have your partner stand straight up against a wall.

B. Put a piece of tape on the wall at the top of your partner's head.

C. Measure the distance between the floor and the tape on the wall.

    1. What is your partner's height?

D. Switch places and have your partner measure you.

    2. What is your height?

    3. What is the average height of the people in your class?

Materials
masking tape
meterstick
paper
pencil

Like any other population, the sizes of your classmates differ. The difference in size between the shortest and tallest organism in a population is called the **range** (**ranj**). What was the *range* of heights in your class?

A virus (**vie**-russ) is a living thing so small that you need a very strong microscope to see it. The virus shown below is enlarged 1,000 times. Four thousand viruses could fit into the period at the end of this sentence.

Range: The difference in size between the tallest and shortest organism in a population.

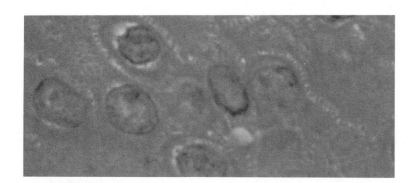

The largest animal is the blue whale. It is over 30 meters (100 feet) long. It weighs over 135,000 kilograms (150 tons). The largest plant is the Sequoia (se-**kwoi**-ah) tree. It is over 90 meters (300 feet) tall and grows in California.

Animals and plants are the sizes they are for a reason. Their size helps them survive. Giraffes can eat foods that other animals are not able to reach. They can also spot their enemies quickly. Their long necks allow them to see very far over bushes and trees. Monkeys can move around quickly because they are so small. Their speed helps them get their food easily and avoid their enemies. Tall trees are able to get the extra sunlight they need because they tower over smaller trees.

MAIN IDEAS

There are many different sizes of plants and animals. Organisms belonging to the same population vary in size. Each organism's size has helped it survive.

QUESTIONS

Write your answers on a sheet of paper.
1. Here are the heights of people in a class.
   a. What is the range of heights in this class?
   b. What is the average height of the students in this class?
2. How has a giraffe's size helped it survive?

Billy 1.8 M	Jake 1.7 M
Sue 1.7 M	Jenny 1.8 M
Stan 1.6 M	Kay 1.6 M

4 CHANGING POPULATIONS

At one time there were two kinds of moths in England. One was dark in color. The other was light. Both moths often landed on trees that were covered by light-colored plants. Which moth had the better chance to survive? When you finish this lesson, you should be able to:

○ Name the word that means differences among members of a population.

○ Tell how a difference in color can help an organism survive.

○ Explain why whole populations can change in such things as color and shape.

You learned that all organisms of the same population are not exactly the same. There are **variations** (var-ee-ay-shuns) in such things as size, shape, and color. Often animals with one *variation* survive better than other animals. This will help you understand why.

Variations: Differences among members of the same population.

ACTIVITY

A. Make a chart like the one shown. Take your chart to the place where your teacher tells you to work.

B. When your teacher says "go," cover one eye with your hand. Begin picking up toothpicks with your other hand. After 20 seconds, your teacher will tell you to stop.

C. Record on your chart the number of red and green toothpicks you picked up.

D. Repeat steps B and C two more times.

1. How many red toothpicks did you pick up all together? how many green toothpicks?

Materials
paper
pencil

trials	number of red toothpicks picked up	number of green toothpicks picked up	total number of toothpicks picked up
1			
2			
3			

Your teacher placed the same number of red and green toothpicks in the grass. You picked more red toothpicks than green ones. Red toothpicks are easier to see in a green background. Suppose these were green insects and red insects. The green ones would be more likely to survive in a grassy place. Their enemies would not be able to find them as easily. Now do you know which color moth in England had a better chance to survive?

Many animals that survive reproduce. The variations that helped them survive are passed on to their newborn. The elephants shown in the drawing below lived on an island. The island had too little food for all the elephants. The smaller elephants survived better than the larger ones. They were able to live on much less food. The smaller elephants reproduced. After a long time the whole population was made up of small elephants.

Often animals with a variation survive better than other animals. Variations that help organisms survive are passed on to the newborn.

QUESTIONS

Write your answers on a sheet of paper.
1. What is the word that means differences among members of the same population?
2. Which bird below has a better chance to survive? Why?

5 DISAPPEARING ORGANISMS

Dinosaurs lived a long time ago. They survived for over sixty million years. Today there is not a single dinosaur alive. Have any other living things disappeared from the earth? Are any living things in danger of disappearing? When you finish this lesson, you should be able to:

○ Name several organisms no longer on the earth.

○ Name several organisms that are in danger of disappearing from the earth.

○ Give two reasons why living things decrease in number or die.

Organisms that no longer live on the earth are called **extinct** (ek-**stinkt**). Dinosaurs are *extinct* animals. Below are pictures of two other extinct animals. Picture 1 shows the Labrador (**lab-bra-door**) duck. Picture 2 shows the passenger pigeon.

More than 170 kinds of animals and 1,700 kinds of plants are becoming rare. Their numbers are decreasing. Some day all of these organisms may be gone. They are all in danger of becoming extinct. They are called **endangered** (en-**dane**-jurd) organisms.

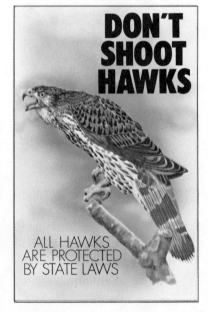

DON'T
SHOOT
HAWKS

ALL HAWKS
ARE PROTECTED
BY STATE LAWS

The animals shown above are *endangered* organisms. They are the bald eagle and grizzly bear. There are many reasons why animals and plants become endangered. A change in the weather over a period of a long time is one reason. Suppose warm temperatures caused the snow and ice around the North and South Poles to melt. Some of the land would become flooded. Many plants and animals would not be able to survive. They would slowly die until none were left.

Human beings sometimes endanger plants and animals. Many buffalo, beavers, and otters were killed so that their skins could be used for clothes. Other animals were killed for food.

Endangered organisms are now protected. It is a crime to hunt them. Is it important to protect animals and plants? What difference does it make to other livings things if an animal or plant becomes extinct? You will learn the answers to these questions in the next unit.

Many plants and animals have become extinct. Others are in danger of becoming extinct. Changes in the environment and human beings have caused animals to become endangered and extinct. Endangered animals are now protected. It is a crime to hunt them.

QUESTIONS

Write your answers on a sheet of paper.

1. What is the difference between extinct organisms and endangered organisms?
2. Name three kinds of organisms that are extinct and three kinds that are endangered.
3. What are two reasons why animals and plants become endangered and extinct?

SOMETHING EXTRA

There is a lake in Scotland called Loch Ness. Many people say there is a creature living in this lake. They call this creature Nessie. The picture you see is supposed to be an underwater picture of Nessie taken in 1934. Scientists have looked for Nessie. They couldn't find a thing. What do you believe? Could Nessie be an animal that we think is extinct but really is not?

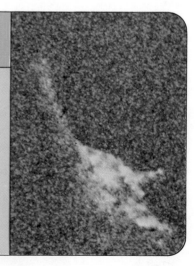

UNIT SUMMARY

A population is a group of the same kind of plants or animals living in the same place. Populations can increase or decrease over periods of time. Members of a population can vary in such ways as size, shape, and color. Variations that help organisms survive are passed on to the newborn.

Living things are suited to their surroundings. They get the things they need to survive from their environment. Some kinds of plants and animals have become extinct. Other kinds are decreasing in number and are in danger of becoming extinct. Laws have been passed to protect endangered organisms.

CHECK YOURSELF

1. A living thing is called a(n) _____.
2. A group of the same kind of living things that live in the same place is a _____.
3. Name three living things whose size has helped them survive.
4. The fast growth of a population is called the _____.
5. The white-yellowish powder or dust found on flowers is called _____.
6. How do insects help fruit trees grow fruit?
7. Why do camels and rabbits live where they do?
8. Differences among members of the same population are called
   a. variations.   c. ranges.
   b. migrations.   d. environments.

9. List four things that a population's size depends on.

10. List four ways that animals make more of their own kind.

11. Name two ways that plants without seeds can make more of their own kind.

12. The word that means to make more of the same kind is

    a. migrate.   c. range.

    b. reproduce.   d. average.

13. Animals no longer living on earth are called _____ organisms.

14. Animals in danger of disappearing from the earth are called _____ organisms.

15. Name two problems that can occur if a population gets too large.

PROJECTS

1. Take care of one or more animals. Birds, gerbils, hamsters, and mice from pet stores are excellent animals to work with. Find out what the animal eats, how it reproduces, and the kind of environment it likes.

2. Find books, pictures, and newspaper clippings of an endangered plant or animal that you would like to learn more about. Find out what is being done to help protect this endangered organism. Make posters so you can share what you have learned with others.

3. Get a tape recorder and a camera. Record different bird songs and calls. Take a picture of each bird you record in its environment. Make a display of the sights and sounds you were able to obtain. Discuss your display with your classmates.

There are four kinds of living things in this picture. Can you name them? They are all found in the same area. They need each other to survive. Do you know why? What do you think would happen to the number of small birds if the insects started dying? Would hawks be affected? Is there a way that dead organisms are helpful to living things? By the time you finish this unit, you will be able to answer these and other questions.

UNIT 6

ANIMAL AND PLANT COMMUNITIES

18

COMMUNITIES AND GREEN PLANTS

1 COMMUNITIES

Imagine walking with a friend through the woods on a cool summer day. You might think "It's nice to be here all alone." But would the two of you really be alone? What other living things might you find around you?

When you finish this lesson, you should be able to:

○ Give the word for all the plants and animals that live in the same place.

○ Give the word that means the place where an organism lives.

○ Name three places where organisms live in a forest and three places where organisms live in a pond.

There are very few places on earth where living things cannot be found. Living things usually live near other living things. All the plants and animals that live in the same place are called a **community** (co-**mew**-nit-tee). There are many kinds of *communities*. Communities of clams, crabs, snails, and algae live in the ocean. Grass and prairie dogs (**prayr**-rhee) are community members of the grasslands or prairie.

Community: All the plants and animals that live in the same place.

Camels and cacti are community members of a desert. Communities of frogs, turtles, pond lilies and fish live in ponds.

Each member of a community lives in a certain place. That place is called a **habitat** (**ha**-bit-tat). There are many *habitats* within a community. In a forest, the soil is the habitat of earthworms and small insects. A salamander's habitat may be an old log. Deer and birds live among the trees and shrubs.

In a pond, cattails grow in the moist soil and mud at the water's edge. Pond lilies are found floating on top of the water. The habitat of frogs, tadpoles, small fish, and insects may be under rocks, under plants, or in the mud.

Communities can also be made of smaller communities. Communities that live in streams and ponds can also be community members of a forest. Communities that live on a sandy beach or seashore also live in part of the community within the ocean. Even a single tree can be the home of a community of many insects, birds, and squirrels.

MAIN IDEAS

All the plants and animals that live in the same place are called a community. Each member of a community has its own habitat, or place where it lives. There are many habitats within the many kinds of communities.

QUESTIONS

Write your answers on a sheet of paper.
1. What is the name for all plants and animals that live in the same place?
2. What is the word that means the place where an organism lives?
3. List three habitats within a forest community and three habitats within a pond community.

2 GREEN PLANTS

Is there something you can do that none of your friends can do? The plants in this picture don't seem to be doing anything. Yet they are doing something very important. They are doing something only green plants can do. When you finish this lesson, you should be able to:

○ List four things that green plants need to be able to make food.

○ Name the word that means the way green plants make food.

Green plants are the only living things that are able to make food. The food making takes place in the green parts of the plant. The corn shown on page 232 was made by the plants' large green leaves. Inside the leaves is a green material called **chlorophyll** (**klor**-oh-fill). The *chlorophyll* gives the green parts of plants their color. It also makes it possible for green plants to make food. But chlorophyll can not do this alone. Other things are needed.

Suppose a green plant is kept in the dark for a few days. Its leaves will begin to lose their green color. Soon after, the plant will die. This tells us that plants need light to make chlorophyll and to stay alive. If you have ever taken care of plants you know that they also need water. The water comes from the soil. Water passes into the roots of a plant, up the stem, and into the leaves.

Plants also need something else. Can you guess what it is? This activity will give you a clue.

Chlorophyll: The green material found in green plants.

A. Cover both sides of a leaf of a healthy plant with petroleum jelly.

1. What happened to the leaf after a few days?

B. Put the plant in a sunny place.

2. What was the leaf prevented from getting?

Materials
healthy plant
petroleum jelly

Carbon dioxide: A gas in the air, which is needed by green plants to make food.

Photosynthesis: The way green plants make food.

Oxygen: A gas in the air, which is given off by the leaves of green plants.

When you covered the leaf with petroleum jelly, you prevented it from getting air. Green plants need a gas in the air to make food. This gas is called **carbon dioxide** (kar-bon die-**ox**-side). The *carbon dioxide* enters the plant through small openings in the leaves. Sunlight provides green plants with the energy to change water and carbon dioxide into food. The way green plants make food is called **photosynthesis** (foe-toe-**sin**-the-sis). *Photo-* means light, and *-synthesis* means to put together. During *photosynthesis*, the leaves give off a gas called **oxygen** (**ox**-eh-jen). It is the *oxygen* in the air that all living things need to live.

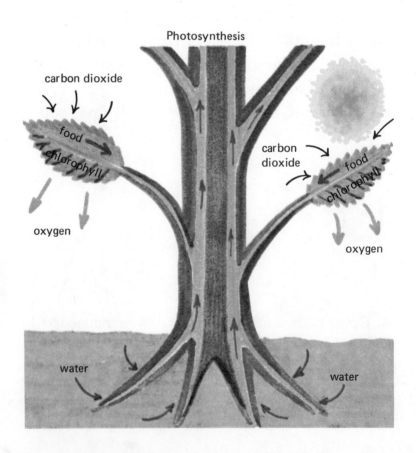

Photosynthesis

carbon dioxide

food

chlorophyll

oxygen

carbon dioxide

food

chlorophyll

oxygen

water

water

Plants need light, chlorophyll, water, and carbon dioxide to make food. The way green plants make food is called photosynthesis. During photosynthesis, leaves give off oxygen. All living things need oxygen to live.

QUESTIONS

Write your answers on a sheet of paper.

1. What four things do green plants need to make food?
2. What word means the way green plants make food?

SOMETHING EXTRA

Forest rangers are people who protect the plants and animals that live in forests. Some forest rangers help animals that are hurt or sick. Others take visitors on nature walks. They teach people about the kinds of living things around them. The forest ranger in the picture is looking at the bark of a tree. She is checking to be sure that the tree is not diseased.

Forest rangers also search for signs of fires. Sometimes fires are started by careless people. If these fires are spotted early, whole communities of plants and animals may be saved, and the beauty of the land will not be destroyed.

CHAPTER 19

THE FOOD CYCLE

1 FOOD MAKERS

All the food in this picture comes from green plants. Do you know the name of each food shown? What part of the plant does each one come from? Have you eaten any green plants today?

When you finish this lesson, you should be able to:

○ Name the word for living things that are able to make their own food.

○ Name a food-making plant found in a prairie, a pond, a desert, and a forest.

Some of the food made by a plant is used to keep the plant alive. The rest is stored in different parts of the plant. The stems, roots, and leaves are all places where food can be found. When you eat carrots, you are eating the roots of a plant. Broccoli is mostly the stem of a plant. Spinach and lettuce are leaves of plants. Peanuts are seeds. A fruit is food that has seeds.

Because green plants can make, or produce, their own food, they are called **producers** (pro-**do**-sirs). The activity on the next page will help you find *producers* in a forest community.

Producers: Living things that are able to make their own food.

237

Materials
notebook
pencil

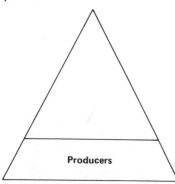

Forest

Producers

A. Draw a chart like the one shown here. Make your chart much larger. Title the chart "Forest."

B. Look for the producers in the picture of the forest shown below.

C. In the space provided on your chart, list all the producers you find.

1. How many producers did you find? What were they?

2. Are any of the animals producers?

238

The trees, grasses, small flowers, and bushes are the producers shown in the drawing of the forest. The deer, squirrels, and fox are not producers. They are not green plants able to make their own food.

In a prairie, the grasses are producers. Cactus plants are producers in a desert. Cattails and pond lilies are food-producing plants in a pond.

In the next lesson you will learn why all communities need producers to survive.

MAIN IDEAS

Green plants are called producers. They are able to make their own food. Some food is used to keep the plant alive. Extra food is stored in the stems, roots, leaves, and seeds. All communities have and need producers to survive.

QUESTIONS

Write your answers on a sheet of paper.
1. What are living things that make their own food called?
2. Name one green plant found in each of the following places: forest, pond, desert.

2 FOOD TAKERS

Frank is having his favorite meal for dinner. Are all the foods in his meal made by producers? Suppose Frank gave his pet rabbit some hamburger? Do you think the rabbit would eat it? When you finish this lesson, you should be able to:

○ Name the word for a living thing that eats plants or animals.

○ Give the names for organisms that eat only plants; only other animals; both plants and animals.

○ Give two examples of each type of organism named above.

Human beings and other animals are not producers. They are not green plants able to make their own food. They get their food by eating plants and other animals. The french fries, hamburger bun, orange juice, and apple that Frank is eating come from producers. French fries are potatoes. Apples are fruit from apple trees. Orange juice comes from oranges, another kind of fruit. Hamburger buns are made from wheat.

Frank's hamburger does not come from a producer. Hamburgers are meat, and meat comes from animals.

A living thing that eats plants or animals is called a **consumer** (kon-**sue**-mer). Human beings and all other animals are *consumers*. Some consumers only eat plants. These animals are called **herbivores** (**err**-bih-vors), or plant eaters. *Herb-* comes from a Latin word that means *grass*. The suffix -*vore* comes from a Latin word that means *to eat*. Cattle, deer, squirrels, mice, rabbits, grasshoppers, and butterflies are *herbivores*.

Some consumers feed only on other animals. These consumers are called **carnivores** (**kar**-nih-vors), or meat eaters. *Carni-* comes from a Latin word that means *meat*. Foxes, coyotes, wolves, lions, seals, and frogs are *carnivores*.

Human beings are consumers that eat both plants and animals. We are called **omnivores** (**om**-nih-vors). *Omni-* means *all*. Bears, chickens, and some turtles are also omnivores.

In the following activity you will be looking at the same forest as on page 238, but with more animals.

Consumer: A living thing that eats plants or animals.

Herbivore: A consumer that eats only plants.

Carnivore: A consumer that eats only animals.

Omnivore: A consumer that eats both plants and animals.

ACTIVITY

Materials

chart (made in
  Chapter 18, lesson 1)
pencil

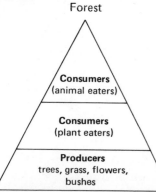

Forest

Consumers
(animal eaters)

Consumers
(plant eaters)

Producers
trees, grass, flowers,
bushes

A. Add two more parts to the chart you made in lesson 1. Label the parts as shown.

B. Look for consumers in the forest shown below.

C. In the spaces provided on your chart, list the consumers that are herbivores. Also list those that are carnivores.

1. How many consumers did you find?

2. Which ones were herbivores?

3. Which ones were carnivores?

4. Did you find any omnivores?

There are six consumers shown in the picture of the forest. The deer, squirrels, and rabbits are herbivores. The fox and lion are carnivores. The bear is an omnivore. Did you list the bear in two places on your chart?

In every community there are producers and consumers. Community charts, like the one you made, can be used to keep track of them. This picture shows how a community chart for a desert might look. Can you think of any other producers or consumers that could be added?

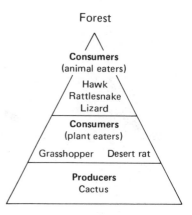

Forest

Consumers
(animal eaters)
Hawk
Rattlesnake
Lizard

Consumers
(plant eaters)
Grasshopper   Desert rat

Producers
Cactus

MAIN IDEAS

A living thing that eats plants or animals is a consumer. Consumers that only eat plants are herbivores. Consumers that only eat animals are carnivores. Consumers that eat both plants and animals are called omnivores.

QUESTIONS

Write your answers on a sheet of paper.
1. What are animal- or plant-eating organisms called?
2. What are the three kinds of plant- and/or animal-eating organisms? Give two examples of each kind.

3 NONGREEN PLANTS

Have you ever seen a grapefruit like the one shown above? What's happening to the grapefruit? What is that greenish-gray coloring? Did a consumer bite into it? When you finish this lesson, you should be able to:

○ Name the word for a living thing that feeds on wastes and dead organisms.

○ Give three examples of this kind of living thing.

○ Tell why the breaking down of dead organisms is important to a community.

Producers and consumers do not live forever. When they die, they begin to change. They begin to rot. We say that they **decay** (de-**kay**). There are tiny organisms in every community that make things *decay*. These living things get their food from wastes and dead organisms. They are called **decomposers** (de-kom-**poz**-ers). The prefix *de-* means to undo. *Compose* means to put together. So *decompose* means to undo what is put together, or to break down. When decomposers feed on dead organisms, they make them decay by breaking them down.

Molds, yeasts and bacteria (bak-**tear**-rhee-ah) are decomposers. They are very tiny non-green plants. They have no chlorophyll, so they cannot carry on photosynthesis to make their own food.

Picture 1 is an enlarged photograph of mold growing on a slice of bread. Molds grow best where it is moist, warm, and dark. The grapefruit shown on page 244 is decaying. A mold is living and growing on it.

Picture 2 shows bacteria. It would take 25,000 bacteria to fit on a line 2.5 centimeters (1 inch) long. Over 2,000 kinds of bacteria are known today. Some are harmful. Some are not. They are found in the air, on our skin, and inside our bodies. Certain bacteria just grow on plants. Others feed on animals. Still others grow just on humans. They all need food to survive.

Yeasts are shown in picture 3. Yeasts live on sugar. You will see how yeast changes a banana when you do the activity on the next page.

Decay: To become rotten.

Decomposer: A living thing that feeds on wastes and dead organisms.

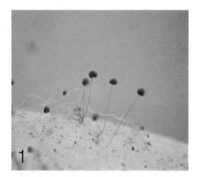

1

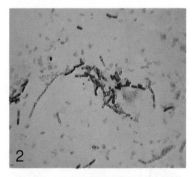

2

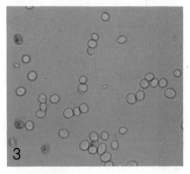

3

Materials
banana
2 plastic sandwich
  bags
yeast

A. Put a slice of banana inside each of the two plastic bags. Sprinkle some yeast on one slice.

B. Close both bags. Mark the bag having the yeast with an *X*.

C. Check both bags every day for five days.

1. Which banana slice showed the most decay? Why?

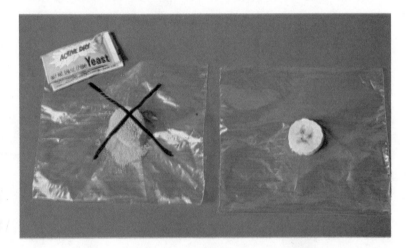

The banana with the yeast decayed faster. The yeast was feeding on the banana and breaking it down. Whenever you see food that is spoiling or rotting, decomposers are at work.

Decomposers are important to a community. Living things break down and decay. As they decay, the ground, air, and water get the materials needed to help other living things grow and stay alive. For example, yeasts, molds, and bacteria all give off carbon dioxide as they feed on wastes and dead organisms. Carbon dioxide is used by green plants to make food.

MAIN IDEAS

Decomposers are living things that get their food from wastes and dead organisms. They decay things by breaking them down. Yeasts, molds, and bacteria are decomposers. When organisms decay, the ground, air, and water get the materials needed to help keep other living things alive.

QUESTIONS

Write your answers on a sheet of paper.
1. What is the name for living things that feed on wastes and dead organisms?
2. Give three examples of the kind of living thing you named in question 1.
3. Why is the decay of dead organisms important to a community?

SOMETHING EXTRA

This is a plant that is a consumer. It adds to the food it produces by trapping insects. When insects walk across the leaves of this plant, the leaves spring shut. Within five to ten days, most of the insect is consumed. Then the leaves open again. The Venus' flytrap is ready for its next meal.

CHAPTER 20
THE PATH OF FOOD

1 FOOD CHAINS

This grasshopper is busy eating grass. Very soon, the grasshopper will be a meal for the bird. The grass is food for the grasshopper. The grasshopper is food for the bird. The food made by the grass has traveled in an interesting path, hasn't it?

When you finish this lesson, you should be able to:

○ Name the words that describe the path that food travels in a community.

○ Tell why decomposers are part of the path of food in a community.

The path that food travels in a community is called a **food chain**. A *food chain* describes how a number of living things depend on each other for food. Most food chains include a green plant, a plant eater, and one or more animal eaters.

Each food chain leads to an animal that is not eaten by other animals. But this is not where a food chain ends. Members of food chains die. When they do, they become food for decomposers. The decomposers break down wastes and dead organisms all along the chain. The broken down materials go back into the soil and water. They are used by producers to make more food.

Food chain: The path that food travels in a community.

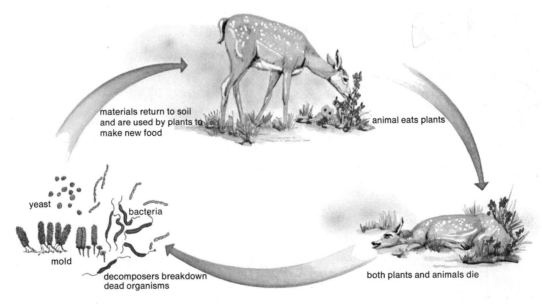

materials return to soil and are used by plants to make new food

animal eats plants

yeast

bacteria

mold

decomposers breakdown dead organisms

both plants and animals die

The grass-grasshopper-bird food chain is not a complete chain. Suppose another animal in the community eats birds. That animal should also be included in the food chain. And decomposers should be added because they feed on grasshoppers, birds, and other members of the chain that die.

Arrows on a community chart show food chains. The chart for a community of grass, grasshoppers, and birds might look like the one shown here.

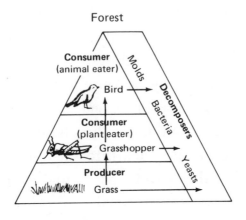

Materials
paper
pencil

A. Read the following chain of events. A butterfly is nibbling on some flowers. A dragonfly eats the butterly. A frog then eats the dragonfly. The next day, a snake eats the frog, and then a hawk eats the snake.

1. Which organisms are the producers? Which are the consumers?

2. List the members of the food chain in correct order. Use arrows to show the path of food.

In the community described in the activity, the grass and flowers were the producers. The butterfly, dragonfly, frog, snake, and hawk were consumers. The butterfly was a plant-eating consumer. The hawk was the last animal consumer in the food chain. The path of food for this community is shown below. What is missing from the diagram?

producer   plant eater   animal eaters

flowers ⟶ butterfly ⟶ dragonfly ⟶ frog ⟶ snake ⟶ hawk

MAIN IDEAS

The path that food travels in a community is called a food chain. Most food chains include a green plant, a plant eater, and one or more animal eaters. Decomposers are also part of every food chain.

QUESTIONS

Write your answers on a sheet of paper.
1. What word describes the path that food travels in a community?
2. Why must decomposers be included in a community's path of food?

2 CONNECTED FOOD CHAINS

A tiny mouse is nibbling on some seeds. A hungry hawk has noticed the mouse. A snake in some tall grass has just seen the same mouse. The hawk dives for the mouse. The snake also moves quietly toward it. A small bird gets frightened at the sight of the diving hawk and starts to chirp. The mouse hears the bird and quickly dashes away. The mouse was lucky this time.

When you finish this lesson, you should be able to:

○ Name the term given to food chains that connect or overlap.

○ Tell what animals that eat other animals are called, and tell what animals that are eaten by other animals are called.

Most communities have many food chains. And most animals in a food chain eat more than one kind of food. Because of this, food chains often connect or overlap. The mouse you just read about was food for both the hawk and the snake. The mouse was part of two different food chains. Food chains that overlap are called **food webs**. Sometimes just two food chains overlap to form a *food web*. Other times a food web has many overlapping food chains.

Food web: Food chains that connect or overlap.

ACTIVITY

A. Study the drawing of the food web shown below.

1. Identify two food chains by listing their members in correct order.

2. Name three organisms that belong to more than one food chain.

Materials
paper
pencil

cat

bird

grasshopper

squirrel

beetle

bat

The food web on page 253 shows that squirrels eat nuts from the tree. Grasshoppers and beetles eat the tree's leaves. Bats and birds eat beetles and grasshoppers. Cats eat squirrels and birds. Five different food chains are involved.

1. nuts → squirrels → cats
2. leaves → beetles → bats
3. leaves → beetles → birds → cats
4. leaves → grasshoppers → bats
5. leaves → grasshoppers → birds → cats

The leaves are the producers in four of the food chains. The beetles, grasshoppers, birds, and bats are each members of two food chains. The cat is part of three chains. The nuts and squirrels belong to just one chain.

Food chains and food webs show us that life really depends on death. One animal eats another, and so on. An animal that kills another animal and then eats it is called a **predator** (pred-ah-tore). The animal that is eaten is called the **prey** (pray).

Predator: An animal that kills another animal and then eats it.

Prey: An animal that is eaten by another animal.

The bird in food chain No. 5 is a *predator* of the beetle. The beetle is the bird's *prey*. Very often a predator becomes another animal's prey. In food chain No. 5 the bird became the prey of the cat. Where do you think people fit into food webs? Are they predators or prey? producers or consumers?

MAIN IDEAS

Food chains that connect or overlap are called food webs. Food chains and food webs show us that life depends on death. An animal that kills another animal and then eats it is a predator. The animal that is eaten is the prey.

QUESTIONS

Write your answers on a sheet of paper.

1. What is the term for food chains that connect or overlap?

2. Look at the food chain below.

   A. Which animals eat other animals? What are animals that eat other animals called?

   B. Which animals are eaten by other animals? What are animals that are eaten by other animals called?

nuts → squirrel → fox → hawk

3 THE BALANCE OF NATURE

Old Tabby is a living mouse trap. She affects the number of mice that live in her community. What do you think will happen to the number of mice if Tabby leaves or dies? When you finish this lesson, you should be able to:

○ Tell how a change in one member of a food chain affects other members in the chain.

○ Give an example that shows the balance of nature.

At one time, scientists believed that deer in Arizona were in danger of being killed off by their predators, the puma, the wolf, and the coyote. They decided to solve this problem by killing the deer's enemies. In less than twenty years, the deer population got much larger. They ate all the green plants around them, including tiny, young trees. This destroyed the forest. The deer could not find enough food. They began to starve to death. Killing the deer's enemies backfired, didn't it?

This story shows that all plants and animals in a community depend upon each other to survive. If something happens to one member of a food chain or food web, other members are affected. Look what happened when the deer's predators disappeared from the food chain. The number of deer increased. But the number of green plants did not. The deer began dying because the forest was no longer able to feed so many of them.

What do you think will happen if the number of frogs in a pond increases? The frogs will eat more insects. The number of insects will decrease. Then the frogs may begin to die because there will not be enough food.

The story of the deer in Arizona shows us that nature has a way of checking, or balancing, itself. The natural predators of the deer could have controlled the number of deer in the community. This is what is meant by the "balance of nature." Usually, predators do not kill any more prey than they need to survive. So there was really no danger of the deer being killed off, as the scientists thought. Without these natural enemies, however, the growing number of deer did not have enough food to survive. So nature stopped the rapid growth of deer by itself. Because of the lack of food, many deer died.

Animals and plants in a community depend upon each other to survive. If something happens to one member of a food chain or web, other members are affected. Nature has its own way of checking, or balancing, changes that occur.

QUESTIONS

Write your answers on a sheet of paper.

1. What would happen to the number of insects in a pond if the number of turtles increased?
2. What would happen to the number of green plants if the number of insects increased?
3. How would nature balance these changes?

SOMETHING EXTRA

This is a picture of one of the most dangerous consumers in the ocean. It is a great white shark. Great white sharks are six to nine meters (twenty to thirty feet) long. They roam through the ocean eating tiny plants and fish of all sizes. Sometimes these sharks swim into the shallow water near ocean beaches. Lifeguards look for the sharks' large fins above the water's surface. When sharks are sighted, swimmers are told to stay out of the water.

21 COMMUNITIES AND PEOPLE

1 PEOPLE AFFECT COMMUNITIES

Would you like to go swimming in this stream? Why do you think the water looks so muddy? Where did the garbage come from? What effect do you think this dirty water has on fish and other living things in the community?

When you finish this lesson, you should be able to:

○ Tell two ways that human beings have harmed communities.

○ Give the name for a scientist who studies communities and their environments.

Human beings also make use of the environment in which they live. Unlike other animals, humans can change an area to meet their own needs. When they do this, other living things in the community may be affected. Sometimes the effects are not good ones. The drawing below shows how wastes from homes and factories may have entered the stream on the opposite page. The papers and cans may have been the leftovers of a Sunday afternoon picnic.

The adding of harmful things to air and water is called pollution. The water in polluted streams is unfit for drinking. It also kills plant and animal life. Suppose the polluted stream water reaches a pond. What do you think would happen to its community members? How would food chains and food webs be affected?

Air pollution also is a problem. Factories and cars give off harmful gases into the air. The insect poisons that farmers spray on their crops also pollute the air. Some of these poisons kill harmless animals as well as insects.

People now realize that they have to find ways to protect communities. We must learn more about how environments and communities affect one another. Scientists who study living things and their environments are called **ecologists** (ee-**kohl**-oh-jists). *Ecologists* study the air, water, and soil. They try to learn all they can about the needs of all organisms. They know that human beings are also part of food chains. When people hurt the rest of the living community, they are also hurting themselves.

Ecologist: A scientist who studies living things and their environments.

MAIN IDEAS

Human beings often affect the environments and communities of other living things. Wastes from factories and homes have polluted streams and ponds. Harmful gases and insect sprays have polluted the air. Ecologists are scientists who study living things and their environments. They look for ways to protect communities of living things.

QUESTIONS

Write your answers on a sheet of paper.
1. What are two ways that human beings have harmed communities?
2. What is the name of the scientist who studies living things and their environments?

2 COMMUNITIES OF HUMAN BEINGS

Do you live in a place like the one shown above? Or are there fewer people and houses in your neighborhood? Do you know the name given to the kind of area you live in? When you finish this lesson, you should be able to:

○ Name and describe the three main kinds of places where humans live.

○ Tell why human beings really belong to two different communities at the same time.

Human beings live in three main kinds of places. The picture on page 264 shows a place where many people live and work. This kind of area is called an **urban area** (**err**-ban). *Urban* means city or town. *Urban areas* usually have large numbers of people, stores, offices, and traffic.

A place near a city where there are homes but few offices and stores is called a **suburban area** (sub-**ber**-ban). Many of the people that work in an urban area live in a *suburban area*. Often suburban areas are called suburbs. Picture 1 below shows a suburb. Notice the rows of one-family homes.

Picture 2 shows an area that has a great deal of wide open space and very few people. This type of place is called a **rural area** (**rur**-al). Very often *rural areas* have many farms. There is usually a post office, a church or temple, and a few stores.

Urban area: A city or town where there are large numbers of people, stores, offices, and traffic.

Suburban area: An area near a city where there are homes but few offices and stores.

Rural area: An area that has a great deal of wide open space and very few people.

**Social community:
A community of
people.**

We have just been describing places where different numbers of people live together. The people living in these places are part of human or **social communities** (so-shall). The word *social* means having to do with people. Remember that there is also a community of plants and other animals within each of the three kinds of *social communities*. This is called a community of nature or a natural community. And human beings are part of this natural community too. For example, large cities have people, dogs, cats, rats, birds, insects, grass, flowers, and trees. Their habitats might be apartment buildings, parks, yards, lots, sidewalk cracks, gardens, and window boxes.

Farms have the same living things found in large cities. They also have horses, cows, chickens, pigs, fruit trees, and vegatable plants. Some farm habitats are barns, stables, chicken coops, and pastures.

MAIN IDEAS

Human beings live in urban, suburban, and rural areas. The people living in these areas are part of the social community. Within each social community, there is also a community of nature. Human beings are also part of this natural community.

QUESTIONS

Write your answers on a sheet of paper.
1. What are the three main kinds of places where humans live? Describe each place.
2. Why do human beings really belong to two different communities at the same time? Give an example in your answer.

SOMETHING EXTRA

Rachel Carson was a person who cared very much about our wildlife and our land. She wrote a book called *Silent Spring*. In this book she said the earth would not have a spring season if people did not stop polluting the land. She was afraid the trees would be bare, and the animals would die. Because of her book laws were passed to protect the land.

UNIT SUMMARY

All the plants and animals that live in the same place are called a community. The green plants in a community are the producers of food. The consumers are animals that feed on producers and other consumers. Decomposers obtain their food from the remains and wastes of plants and animals.

A food chain describes the path of food in a community. A food web is a group of connected food chains. If something happens to one member of a food chain, other members are affected.

People are also part of communities. We share our communities with other living things.

CHECK YOURSELF

1. Bacteria, molds, and yeasts are all examples of
   a. producers.   c. decomposers.
   b. consumers.   d. green plants.
2. All the plants and animals that live in the same place make up a _____.
3. List the names of the three kinds of consumers.
4. Food chains that overlap or connect are called _____ _____.
5. Scientists who study living things and their environments are called _____.
6. A living thing that eats plants or animals is a _____.

7. The name given to the way green plants make food is
   a. decay.
   c. producer.
   b. photosynthesis.
   d. chlorophyll.

8. List the names for the three main kinds of places where humans live.

9. An animal that kills another animal and then eats it is called a
   a. predator.
   c. prey.
   b. food chain.
   d. decomposer.

10. The place where a living thing lives within a community is called a _____.

PROJECTS

1. Locate a community of living things near your home or school. Some habitats may be lawns, parks, streams, or even a vacant lot that has plants and insects. Try to identify the producers, consumers, and decomposers. Write their names or draw them on a community chart. Use arrows to show food chains or webs.

2. Cut out pictures of producers and consumers from magazines. Arrange the pictures on posters to show different food chains. Display the posters side by side in your classroom. Use string to show where food chains displayed on the different posters may overlap from food webs.

3. Study your community to find ways in which people are changing the environment. Find out how the changes are affecting the plants and animals that share the community with you. Report your findings to the class.

4 crayons = 38.6 grams

THINK METRIC

4 milliliters
of milk

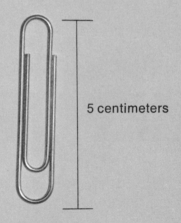

5 centimeters

1 battery =
87.8 grams

3 jacks = 5.5 grams

4 of these = about 1 liter

13.75 centimeters

GLOSSARY/INDEX

Community (co-**mew**-nit-tee): all the plants and animals that live in the same place, 228–229, 230–231/food chains in, 248–249, 250–251, 268

Compound machine (**kom**-pound): a machine made of two or more simple machines, 168–171

Condensation (kahn-den-**say**-shun): the change of a gas into a liquid, 125–126

Cone-shaped mountains, 19–22

Conserve (kon-**serv**): to save, or not waste, energy, 178, 179

Conservation, of land, 43; of wildlife, 43

Consumer (kon-**sue**-mer): a living thing that eats plants or animals, 241, 268

Continental drift (con-tin-**nen**-tal **drift**): the idea that the continents are moving, 8

Convex lens (**kon**-vex): a lens that is thicker in the middle than at the edges, 79–81

Core: the center layer of the earth, 5, 44

Coyotes, 241, 257

Crust: the thin, solid, outer layer of the earth, 3, 5, 44/cracks in, 14–17; plates of, 11, 13, 44

Cumulus clouds (**kue**-mew-lus): patches of puffy white clouds, 96, 98, 117

Curved glass, 73–76; *See also* Lens(es).

Curved mirrors, 65–68; focusing of light with, 67, 68, 75

Decay (de-**kay**): to become rotten, 245

Decomposer (de-kom-**poz**-er): a living thing that feeds on wastes and dead organisms, 244–245, 246–247, 249–251, 268

Deer, 206, 230, 239, 241, 243, 257, 258

Diesel engines, 175

Dinosaurs, 220, 221

Dome mountains: mountains formed by forces under the surface of the earth lifting the crust, 26

Drizzle (**driz**-uhl): very small drops of slowly falling rain, 118

Dust, clouds and, 126

Earth, core of, 5, 44; crust of, 3, 5, 44; mantle of, 4, 5, 11, 44

Earthquake (**erth**-kwake): a sudden movement in the earth, 14, 15–18/safety precautions during, 18

Earthquake belt, 15, 21

Ecologist (ee-**kohl**-oh-jist): a scientist who studies living things and their environments, 263

Electric cars, 179

Electric energy, 174

Elephants, 218

Endangered (en-**dane**-jurd): in danger of becoming extinct, 221–224

Energy (**en**-err-jee): the ability to do work, 172–173, 174–179/from coal, 175, 177; conservation of, 178, 179; electric, 174; from gas, 175, 177; machines and, 176–179; need for new sources of, 177, 179; from oil, 175, 177; solar, 68, 178; from steam, 175; of water, 174, 175; in wind, 174, 175

Environment (en-**vie**-ran-ment): everything in the surroundings that affects an organism's life, 205/of animals, 204–207; of plants, 208–211

Erosion (ee-**row**-shun): the carrying away of rocks and soil from one place to another, 33, 44/by glaciers, 35–38; reduction of, 34; by rivers, 32–34

Evaporation (ee-vap-pore-**ray**-shun): the changing of a liquid into a gas, 125

Extinct (ek-**stinkt**): does not exist anymore, 221, 223, 224

Eyeglasses, 81

Fault: a place where the rocks along the sides of a crack have moved, 16, 17, 25, 26

Fault-block mountains: mountains formed by the cracking and tilting of rocks along faults, 25, 26

Machine: anything that makes work easier, 144–145, 146–147/compound, 168–169, 170–171; and energy, 176–179; problems caused by, 177, 179; simple, 145–167

Machine tool, 147

Machinists, work done by, 147

Magma (**mag**-ma): red-hot melted rock under the earth's surface, 20–21, 26

Mantle (**man**-till): a very thick layer of the earth found under the crust, 4, 5, 11, 44

Metals, 3; iron, 5; nickel, 5

Meteorologists (me-tee-or-**ahl**-oh-jists): scientists who study the weather, 95; work done by, 98

Mid-ocean ridges (mid-**oh**-shun **rij**-jez): chains of mountains formed near the center of the oceans, 11–13

Migration (my-**gray**-shun): the movement of animals from one place to another, 206–207

Minerals (**min**-err-als): materials rocks are made of, 29

Mirrors, curved, 65–68; and images, 61–64; and reflection of light, 56–60

Molds, 245–247

Monkeys, 214

Mountains, 23; Appalachian, 24; Black Hills of South Dakota, 26; building of, 23–26; cone-shaped, 19–22; dome, 26; fault-block, 25, 26; folded, 24, 26; mid-ocean ridges, 11–13; Sierra Nevada, 25; volcanic, 19–22; weathering of, 27–30

Movable pulley: a pulley that moves with the load, 158, 159

Movement of continents, 6–9

Muir, John, 43

Nature, balance of, 256–259; community of, 266

Oceans, spreading floors of, 12, 13; mountain chains near centers of, 11–13

Oil, 3; energy from, 175, 177

Omnivore (**om**-nih-vor): a consumer that eats both plants and animals, 241

Opticians, work done by, 81

Organism (**ore**-ga-niz-um): a living thing, 185

Otters, 222

Oxygen (**ox**-eh-jen): a gas in the air, which is given off by the leaves of green plants, 234

Passenger pigeon, 221

Periscope (**pehr**-riss-scope): an instrument that uses two mirrors to see around corners, 59, 60

Photosynthesis (foe-toe-**sin**-the-sis): the way green plants make food, 234, 235

Physical weathering (**fizz**-eh-kahl): the changing of a rock's size and shape as it breaks down, 29

Plants, 184–187; cactus, 210, 230, 239; cattails, 230, 239; endangered, 221–224; environments of, 208–211; green, food-making process in, 232–235, 246; growth of, things needed for, 208–211, 233; and physical weathering, 29, 30; pond lilies, 230, 239; reproduction in, 196–199; sizes of, differences in, 212–215; Venus' flytrap, 247

Plates (**playts**): large sections of the earth's crust, 11, 13, 44

Pollen (**pahl**-len): a yellowish powder made by the anthers of a flower, 197

Pollination, 197–199

Pollution (po-**loo**-shun): the adding of harmful things to air or water, 177, 179, 260–263

Population (pop-you-**lay**-shun): a group of the same kind of organisms that live in the same place, 186 ; changes in size of, reasons for, 202; counting size of, method for, 188–191; human, 186

Population explosion (ex-**splo**-shun): the rapid growth of a population, 202, 203

PHOTO CREDITS

Unit 6: p. 226—S. J. Krasemann/Peter Arnold; p. 227—Tom Brakefield/Bruce Coleman; p. 228—Caroll/Peter Arnold; p. 229—*left* Runk/Schoenberger/Grant Heilman; *right* Phil Dotson/ DPI; p. 232—Grant Heilman; p. 235—U.S. Forest Service; p. 241—Runk/Schoenberger/Grant Heilman; p. 244—W. H. Hodge/Peter Arnold; p. 245—Runk/Schoenberger/Grant Heilman; p. 247—Runk/Schoenberger/Grant Heilman. p. 254—Grant Heilman; p. 257—Phil Dotson/DPI; p. 259—Rodney Fox/Black Star; p. 260—Ted Rozumlski/EPA-Documerica; p. 262—USDA Photo; p. 264—Michos Tzovaras/Editorial Photocolor Archives; p. 265—*left* Grant Heilman; *right* Lizabeth Corlett/DPI; p. 266—*left* Susan Szasz/EPA—Documerica; *right* Grant Heilman; p. 267—UPI.

ART CREDITS

Howard Asch, pages 184, 218, 222, 249, 252, 253
Howard Berelson, pages 201, 219, 220
Lisa Bonforte, pages 248, 256
Jane Clark, pages 146, 156
Eulala Conners, pages 230, 238, 242, 258
Marie De John, page 261
Claude Martinot, pages 4, 8, 9, 11, 12, 15, 49, 53, 57, 58, 59, 62, 66. 70, 74, 83, 84, 87, 89, 104, 105, 106, 110, 113, 121, 122, 123, 126
Stella Ormai, pages 10, 51
Jerry Zimmerman, pages 6, 14, 64, 112, 134, 170, 182–183, 208, 237, 270, 271